BOOKS BY

J. Gregory Conway

CONWAY'S TREASURY OF FLOWER ARRANGEMENTS
(1953)

FLOWERS: THEIR ARRANGEMENT
(1940)

FLOWERS: EAST-WEST
(1938)

These are Borzoi Books published in New York by
ALFRED A. KNOPF

CONWAY'S

TREASURY OF

FLOWER ARRANGEMENTS

CONWAY'S
TREASURY OF
FLOWER
ARRANGEMENTS

BY

J. GREGORY CONWAY

Photography by Julian Hiatt

ALFRED·A·KNOPF: NEW YORK, 1953

L. C. CATALOG CARD NUMBER: 53–6847

THIS IS A BORZOI BOOK
PUBLISHED BY ALFRED · A · KNOPF, INC.

FIRST EDITION

PREFACE

HE PRINCIPLES of flower arrangement have been presented in complete detail in my two previous books, *Flowers: Their Arrangement* and *Flowers: East-West*. The material presented here goes beyond these basic guiding principles in flower arrangement to the creative expressing of ideas. As a result of artificially imposed restrictions and the persistence of a certain amount of misinformation, flower arrangers all too frequently display a lack of initiative and a hesitancy to give way to self-expression. It is to encourage the free play of the creative imagination in flower arrangement—always guided by sound æsthetic principles—that this book has been written.

Rules that are offered as guides for beginners in flower arrangement tend to standardize the art. When one is skilled enough, however, and has sufficient knowledge and ingenuity to create something different, variations are highly desirable. Indeed, it is often necessary to violate rules in order to express definite ideas. The challenge of deviation from rules may well result in that distinction which forever sets apart the work of the most talented artists from that of less creative persons.

Flower arrangement is a universal art. For this reason, and out of deference to my students in many lands, the plant materials used in the preparation of this book present a wide range of geographic varieties. Even so, many of the plant materials have been grown in my own garden.

I am indebted to Elinor Wallace Hiatt for her invaluable creative contributions in the preparation of this book.

For horticultural notes, I wish to thank Alice Lorraine Kennon. For the use of their containers, as well as for co-operation in other ways, I am grateful to Bernice Lutz, Marie Hargrove, my sister Claire, and Melvin Bussey.

CONTENTS

FLOWER ARRANGEMENTS [*continued*]

CONWAY'S

TREASURY OF

FLOWER ARRANGEMENTS

THE ART OF

FLOWER ARRANGING

THE DEVELOPMENT of flower arranging in the Occidental world has had little or no help from the artists who work in other mediums. It is coming of age by means of its own inspiration. Its growth in America, as well as in other Occidental countries, has been tremendous in recent years; and although in the West it never can be considered a cult—as in the Orient, where religious symbolism has determined the course of this art—it nevertheless has attained here a stature of great significance. Since nature is its own reason for being, it is no wonder that to us of the West the art of flower arranging is a soul-satisfying expression akin to the deep religious experience of the Orient.

In countries where the art is free from the restrictions imposed by Oriental design, the floral artist employs as his mediums the same transient materials as are used by the Oriental. But because the underlying purpose of his creations is wholly at variance with the fundamental reasons that impel the Oriental designer, he reaches a different end. The divergence in these basic concepts must be understood; for it is that unlikeness that makes possible a rich future for Western floral art.

Two ideas have governed Oriental floral design: the motivating force and the method of expression. From the outset the Oriental was actuated by religious belief and precept. In the early stages of the art the extrinsic beauty of the design seems to have been a minor consideration; the floral material itself was of primary importance as the instrument of religious interpretation. Repeated manipulations of flowers and foliage in these early beginnings brought the discovery that floral materials are beautiful in themselves, apart from precept, and that their true loveliness could be revealed completely only through studied arrangement—the arrangement remaining, it should be noted, a purely religious representation. To depict this symbolism the Oriental used a very simple method of expression: he treated his floral materials realistically. He selected them, in the first place, for their native fitness to the ideas they were to represent; then he arranged them after the manner of their growth, since their growth, in itself, suggested a universal idea. Out of this primitive design of the early classical school evolved the later thought of interpreting life in pattern: creating floral designs as representations of actual landscape units; delineating ideas as literally as possible.

The West has experienced nothing in art to compare with this binding symbolism of the Orient. Never has there been a great teacher or a great movement to build toward a national acceptance of the art of flower arranging, which has been practiced primarily for decorative purposes, as one means of obtaining prettiness within the home. A pleasing combination of attractive flowers was all that one wanted; a nice bouquet to set in a vase satisfied the need for home decoration. Although a spreading awareness of art principles has started the West toward an examination of its flower arrangements and an appraisal of its standards of floral art, a general comprehension of the æsthetic basis of floral design has been long delayed. One example will illustrate the need of artistic understanding: the extravagance of color and materials in Occidental designs, much like the style of early flower paintings. No restrictions of any kind existed to curb the early designer. Such limitations as Westerners have come to impose, however, have been determined only by their sense of fitness and not in conformity to any established code. They still retain the idea of prettiness but are reaching out toward a concept that is more satisfying than mere attractiveness. They work freely toward creative expression, deftly fashioning their living material into a portrayal of their personal, and perhaps momentary, ideas. They paint with flowers—not realistically, not literally, but imaginatively. It is this untrammeled imagination that sets them forever apart from the Oriental designers. For the Orientals were bound by ancient beliefs that had crystallized into dogma; they were caught fast in the pattern of spent time. But the Western creator can move freely, since art knows not rules, but principles.

The current trend in interior design is toward simplification. Furniture, glass and china, rug patterns—all are built after the architectonic ideal of functional beauty attained through the spare use of line. Flower arrangements, also, no longer exhibit the massive abundance in which the past generations took pride. Because I recognized the general need of simplicity I wrote *Flowers: East-West*. At that time, I felt that a working knowledge of Oriental line composition would restrain Occidental enthusiasm for mass alone, and that both the East and the West might profit by this fusion. Indeed the West has. Not so the East. Unfortunately, Japanese flower arrangement is so completely cluttered with centuries-old rules and traditions that it has remained stereotyped. The art, once so admirable for its classic restraint, is currently confused. The Japanese have worked for so many centuries in rigid conformity to their rules that now, when they attempt a new creation, they are unable to feel their way to originality in design.

Western followers of floral art, then, should be awakened to the tragedy that can befall any art based solely on rule and restriction. There is, for example, no real reason for the idea that dark flowers must always be the center of interest and placed low; or the assumption that centerpieces must always be horizontal; or the precept that every arrangement must be one and one-half times the height or width of the container. All these practices are the result of imposed rules. Any form of art that becomes rigidly cast into set rules has become decadent. Fortunately this decadence can sometimes give way to newer expressions of individuality. The eighteenth century illustrates this fact. The rigid rhythms of Alexander Pope and his followers were followed by the originality and the freedom of the Romantic movement, by the personal and unrestrained poetry of Burns and Wordsworth and Byron.

The foundation of a pleasing flower arrangement is a knowledge of art elements in design freely manipulated. These elements are basic to all the visual arts and are defined as line, form, texture, pattern, and color.

By LINE is meant the general direction that the arrangement assumes. The dominant line should be suggested by the plant material to be arranged. Lines give strong emotional quality to the floral design.

The vertical is the line of strength and spiritual aspiration, hence its use in Gothic styles of architecture. The sculptor uses this line as advantageously for achieving a spiritual quality in religious figures as for expressing fixed purpose or vigorous achievement in human activity. In somewhat the same manner as other artists select their basic line, the floral artist is guided in his choice of line by the need that the design must satisfy. Since the line structure usually is suggested by the background of the room or the object upon which the arrangement is to be placed, any narrow, restrained columns or vertical panels would of themselves indicate to the floral composer that the basic idea of the arrangement be an erect style.

The horizontal line is considered static, a line of peace and repose. It becomes the foreground, the middle distance, or the background line. Elongated surfaces and low, flat planes within the home interior propose to the floral designer the use of the reclining line.

Curved lines usually imply completion, because the line tends to return to itself. An unfinished or a broken curve frequently is more beautiful than the full circle, because the eye can escape confinement; the imagination will supply the details that the designer has merely suggested. Curves serve to their best advantage when rounded furniture or radiating lines are background features.

Combinations or segments of these lines give resultant shape or FORM to the arrangement. These basic forms are few and simple: the pyramid, the cone, the sphere, and the cube. Since all form is three-dimensional, the flower arrangement must be manifestly three-dimensional. All too frequently floral designs look like two-dimensional cut-outs. While one who paints flowers must achieve his contours through illusion, the flower arranger has the privilege of working in the third dimension. In the individual forms of the blossoms, together with their natural coloring, he has, in effect, a combination of the mediums of both the sculptor and the pigment artist. By careful placing of individual flowers at varied angles and in recessive planes, he secures his feeling of depth and molded form.

TEXTURE is an element noticeable in the art of flower arranging. One is aware that it exists, but it need not be overemphasized, for it is possibly the least important element in the flower art. Texture is the tactile appearance of plant material. The surface of the flower or leaves may be delicate or heavy or shiny or striated. When similar textures are combined, the design achieves tactile unity. Often, however, one wants a tactile contrast, as in a combination of smooth, leathery leaves with a hairy surface.

PATTERN is actually the wholeness or the entirety of the floral composition, including its spaces and masses. No floral arrangement can exist in emptiness. It sits on a base against some kind of background, if only a wall at a distance. This pattern, or composition, is not made solely of plants. It contains also the empty spaces between the flowers, the stems, and the leaves; and these voids are as much a part of the pattern as are the flowers. The plant material has been carefully set to provide for these voids, so that each flower and leaf may be secure in its own relative importance. Thus there is a design of masses and space set within an imaginary frame against a background. Pattern is a most important element in this visual art and should be emphasized in floral design.

Undoubtedly the COLOR element of design is of great interest to the arranger. Color appreciation of a sort is common to everyone, though it is not always accompanied by a technical understanding. Without color a design may be beautiful, as in a black and white photograph. This same subject, if photographed in color, becomes radiantly lovely. Color enhances floral design in much the same fashion. So much has been written about color that the theory, as well as its application or appreciation, is usually sufficiently clear to the flower arranger.

A knowledge of basic color harmonies as practiced in the West, together with good taste, is the prerequisite for deft color execution. Emotionally, color is most interesting. Red is possibly the only color having a universal connotation. To primitive man it represented fire. At first fire meant danger, possibly death. Later man learned to control it to his own needs, and it then came to mean warmth and comfort. Red, then, can be dangerous or very pleasing.

Certain color combinations in the Orient are used symbolically to denote positive and negative forces. Masculine and feminine colors must be portrayed simultaneously. Vivid orange and pale pink would be a possible combination to the Oriental; but to Western eyes this combination is atrocious. White is used for mourning in the Asiatic countries since it suggests that a soul has ascended into light. In the Occident black is worn to denote the passing of a loved one. I mention these usages so that the reader may understand that color application varies from race to race. Within any social culture there may be present several overlappings of color application, made possible through study and broad understanding of basic design. While the untutored, perhaps, may view the intricate color harmony of a Persian rug as a jumbled discord, we prize its richness. For one must be conditioned to color. American designers usually work in complementary or analogous color harmonies, together with their variants, because we have been educated to these combinations. No æsthetic principle, however, states that these combinations and these alone are beautiful. If, for example, a woman enters a Mexican arrangement in a competitive flower show, she should be free to create her composition according to her own ideas, guided always by basic principles of design. The conventional American arrangement would call for warm, analogous colors of red, orange, and yellow. The Mexican designer, on the contrary, would use orange and cerise, with marigolds, perhaps, and bougainvillea. The beauty of his creation we would term primitive simply because we have not been trained to appreciate it. If our hypothetical woman of the competitive flower show understands Mexican ideas of color combinations, why should she not build her arrangement to conform to Mexican standards? There can be no binding restrictions in flower arrangement. The floral artist should be as free to manipulate color as is the modern painter. What may be proper and pleasing in one country may at first be perplexing in another. The use of color, in the final analysis, resolves itself into the matter of taste. We reach out for all beauty; we select from foreign ideas that which pleases us; we choose and adapt. Always must we be restrained not by rules but by taste. We should not attempt any wide-scale appropriation of foreign beauty that is entirely antagonistic to our taste; but we must recognize the fitness of exotic color in exotic settings. We should also concede the use of such harmony in our own civilization if the proper setting has been established and if the strange harmony can express the designer's true purpose more surely than can the conventional colors. In other words, our attitude toward the use of color today should be open-minded.

In addition to the elements of design which are basic, there are many principles of design, such as balance, repetition, contrast, and the like. Of these, BALANCE is the most important in the art of flower arranging. Balance is the grouping of the plant materials within the pattern so that the general effect is pleasing to the eye and the weight is equalized. This achievement of balance does not mean that the form of the design must be symmetrical.

Anyone can make pleasing compositions by the observance of a few elements and that important principle of design known as balance. Basically, a knowledge of line, an awareness of pattern by the proper employment of spaces and masses, and the control of the instrument of color, together with a steady sense of balance, are sufficient. One should not even then become so completely absorbed in the worry of overdefinition that he loses his creative self-expression.

An overemphasis on containers has interposed a needless difficulty between the designer and his fragile art. Fundamentally the container is nothing more than a receptacle for holding water. But it should help to create a pleasing sense of proportion in the over-all composition of the arranged plant material, if and when the viewer judges the two as if isolated in space. On the other hand, when a floral design is to function in a background setting, as most such arrangements do, the whole composition counts in relation to its setting.

Much has been written on the care and treatment of flowers. Unconfirmed statements and old wives' tales have contributed much misinformation. In *Flowers: East-West,* I included Oriental methods of plant preservation as practiced in those countries. Little did I realize then that many of my Western readers would go to extremes in attempting to use such methods. The Oriental employment of sugar, vinegar, and numerous spices in an attempt to prolong the life of flowers was presented merely as historical information, primarily to authenticate the purism of Oriental art and technique.

As a practical exponent of floral art, I suggest two preservative methods that will suffice for the floral kingdom in general. One is the almost complete defoliation of the blossoming stalk; and the other is complete immersion of the plant material: flower, stalk, and all. The latter method is especially adapted to branches or to individual leaves. In the defoliation method, the stem end is cut and the stalk is placed in deep water. Plant materials needing complete immersion will react in many instances even more rapidly than those requiring to be placed only in deep water. They soon become very crisp because of their horizontal position. It is not necessary to leave flowers in water as long as is generally supposed.

Materials so treated are now ready for arranging. When they are placed in the containers, the actual depth of water is governed by two factors: the length of the stem and the cell structure. One should not put a long-stemmed rose in an inch of water, since such a limited quantity of water cannot fill the cell tissues. But a long gladiolus stem, with an altogether different structure, can exist easily in a one-inch water supply. The floral artist, then, can profit by botanical knowledge. Should one or two placements in the final arrangement have wilted after several hours, do not disturb the entire design, but remove the offenders, recut the stem end, and again immerse completely or sink the stem deeply, depending upon the plant material. When the flower, leaf, or stalk is firmly erect, it can be returned to the design. This process rarely needs repeating. Never change the water unless the odor becomes objectionable; replenish the water content as it is used up by the arranged materials.

The transient life of flowers is the very thing that gives expressiveness and interprets a philosophy of life. To attempt to preserve flowers indefinitely is self-defeating and unæsthetic.

Arrangements of dried materials can be as satisfying as patterns developed from living plants, if used appropriately. Such materials also express a phase of nature; and when arranged with a specific idea in mind they may provide austere beauty for a quiet room. In the more northerly climates the dried wisp of grass and roadside dock tossed by the strong winds of outdoors and perhaps destroyed by the violence of nature can be very beautiful, within the confines of the protective home shelter, when arranged to suggest those very forces which can work such ugly destruction in actuality. In the tropics the dried palm frond or spent spathe, hurricane-torn, relives that moment of the restlessness of the elements. All these arrangements I suggest as a part of the panorama of life.

The knowledge required to grow living things and the love of such growth give stability and background to those who wish to excel in floral art. Gardening knowledge can contribute much toward a richer understanding of life. Without this intimate knowledge of nature, floral design lacks the warm breath of true art. It is quite possible without horticultural experience to achieve both pleasing and spectacular design, but it takes the knowledge of dirt gardening to give a spirit of understanding to the arranging art. Book knowledge alone is not enough; but experience with nature's surrounding and encompassing beauty is needed.

In the gardening art, elements of design identical with those used in floral arrangements should be employed with understanding. Line and form affect the dominant style and æsthetic effect of the garden. Its textures afford pleasing variation by the combination of plant material. Its pattern presents the arrangement of masses and spaces, the silhouette of trees tossed against the sky. Its color offers a rainbow of delight when rotated seasonally by plantings harmoniously chosen. And lastly, the principle of balance will give stability and repose to the garden.

It was the growing of plant materials that first stimulated in me the desire to produce floral designs. Nature at random is a magnificent sight, but it, too, can stand refining. A branch that makes for shelter, and water that satisfies thirst can just as easily become food for the soul in a flower arrangement. To take this bounty and employ it to satisfy spiritual needs is the very essence of the art of living.

In this book I have tried to help the arranger. To that end I have included descriptions of the plant material selected for portraying the art of arrangement. Should your interest lie primarily in arranging flowers, you might wish to know more about general characteristics and methods of growth of some of the material used. Should you be primarily a horticulturist, such information may prove beneficial. Many times plant material common in one area is completely unknown in another region of similar climatic and growing conditions, solely because it has not been introduced and no one knows of it. This book supplies some of the information that may lead to such introduction. It has been planned in a purposefully simple yet informative manner.

If you are a flower arranger, your art will be strengthened by a knowledge of horticulture. One experience gives balance to the other; and the flower arranger fortunate enough to control his own source of supply is a privileged individual indeed.

The following pages offer ideas of design and suggested presentation for the plant material described. They also provide the cultural hints for its growth, together with other useful and interesting information about the plant. By such a presentation I hope to give inspiration to those who are either gardeners or flower arrangers, or both.

I have selected a wide variety of plant materials and flowers which lend themselves to artistic expression. Some are startling, others modest; but all play a part in providing the designer or the grower with inspiration. Certain accessory objects which nature supplies abundantly, although inanimate, can express deft beauty. Rocks, driftwood, branches, dried materials, and the like can contribute to the appeal of the design or can even supply the basis of the design. Seen daily, unnoticed because of their familiarity as weeds or rocks or stumps, they have been overlooked as possibilities for floral design through the designer's lack of experience in this medium of expression. Because of my inclusion of these materials, this book does not conform to the standard pattern of books on either floral art or floral culture.

The pictorial presentation takes up each plant material or medium featured. It usually illustrates the subject alone with its own foliage. A companion picture on the same page discloses the identical material rearranged and purposefully including additional material. These two companion illustrations, in black and white, accompany one large plate showing the featured subject in full color. Sometimes this colored portrayal presents the subject alone or, again, with other materials, depending upon what I consider to be the most desirable projection of the subject. A full page of text accompanies each of the one hundred color plates. In this manner you are introduced, perhaps, to unfamiliar plants; others known to you may now, it is hoped, be appraised with an enriched understanding.

Every illustration in this volume is practically planned. The only floral subjects not in water are those whose full life span is not dependent upon water. There is no artificial distortion at any time of any of the plant material presented. In only three plates has wire been used and then only to support lifeless material. These are the black magnolia leaves in the cockscomb presentation, the feathers with the pelargonium presentation, and the skeletonized avocado leaves with petunias.

The pin-type holder is used in low bowls, and folded wire mesh in the more vertical containers. Segments of branches support the flowers in the clear glass vertical containers. None of the usual gadgets, such as string, tape, putty, pins, or other props have been employed. The simpler the mechanical approach, the purer the finished expression.

NOTE

FULL DESCRIPTIONS of the arrangements

shown in the black-and-white illustrations

are grouped in alphabetical sequence begin-

ning on page 315.

Acanthus

HE ACANTHUS is a beautifully decorative perennial. From the first early spring growth of the leaves to that moment in late summer when the foliage must be cut away, the plant is easily the dominant feature in its garden environment. The large leaves, often eighteen or more inches in length and half as wide, are deeply cleft, with segments in some varieties that suggest the indentations of the thistle. The foliage is almost entirely basal. Borne on short stalks, the leaves curl toward their tips in great, sweeping curves that lift a portion of their length edgewise above their flat center.

It must have been this manner of growth that inspired the Greeks to use the acanthus leaf in the capital of the Corinthian columns. Their genius for observation would show them in the native pliancy of the leaf those specific features essential to architectural support: the pinnæ to define sharply the edges of the capital; the broad leaf folded forward and down to offer generous support for weight. The curl of the leaf particularly is noticeable in the architectural motifs of the Greeks.

The acanthus should be planted more generally than at present in areas where it does not require winter mulching. It needs a rich, light soil with good drainage. While it is very useful for background planting in borders to create a subtropical effect, it must not be shaded. It does best in open ground with infrequent irrigation; except for the summer blooming period, much water is fatal. The flowers with their stiff bracts are closely packed on tall, strong stalks. Though their tones range from dull white through beige to rose or purple, the form and the texture are more distinctive than the colors. Coarse, almost rough, the spikes are suited to large, spectacular arrangements set against a plain, heavy background such as burlap. The tips are weak; total immersion will stiffen them sufficiently to retain their position.

Acanthus

Acanthus and Melianthus Major

ACANTHUS

The use of acanthus flowers with canna leaves illustrates the fine harmony created through a felicitous combination of unrelated material. The symmetrical overlapping of the canna leaves, turned to display their strong central vein, builds a sweeping vertical that complements the straight lines of the acanthus. The color relationship between the bracts of the acanthus and the leaves of the red canna, rather than the green, is furthered by the richness of the pottery container whose serrated edge suggests the regularity of the flower points.

Agapanthus

THE AGAPANTHUS is a handsome member of the lily family whose comeliness beguiled early fanciers into naming it the lily-of-the-Nile. It had, unfortunately, no connection with Cleopatra, since it came not from Egypt but from South Africa. In warmly temperate areas the agapanthus thrives in the garden, where it likes a rich soil, well drained, with much water during the growing and blooming periods. It will succeed in sunny locations, but responds best to light shade. In areas too cold for all-year garden residence it may be planted in a tub, then moved outdoors for the summer. When cultivated in this manner, it needs liberal allowances of liquid manure, for it is a heavy feeder.

The potted agapanthus makes a highly decorative accent for porch or terrace. In the open garden it is particularly lovely in rows. The foliage is richer than that of most tuberous plants, with long, narrow strap leaves in shapely clusters that are brightly green throughout the year. Insufficient watering will cause loss of foliage, but normal care ensures a generous ground cover. The blossoms are borne on strong stalks considerably taller than the leaves. Each flower head is an umbel of long, slender, funnel-shaped florets radiating on delicate stems from the top of the stalk and standing far enough above the mass of leaves to seem almost to float in space.

Both white and blue varieties are exquisite in arrangements. The star cluster is displayed to best advantage in a simple design, usually a very few umbels set among their own leaves. When grouped with other plant material, the agapanthus should be the center of interest. The flowers last well if the water in the container is shallow. Pick them when only the outer rim of the cluster is showing its funnels. Others will open gradually, always toward the center, with a day-by-day change in design that is lovely to watch.

Agapanthus

Agapanthus and Aralia Leaves

AGAPANTHUS

This triangular pattern exemplifies the value of space in floral composition. The massing of blue and white agapanthus at the base provides the
stability necessary to support the height of the morea placement. Three
long stems of morea, bare except for terminal flowers and bud, complete
the contour of the pyramid. The exquisite container of Persian porcelain
displays a wealth of ornamentation whose delicacy is unusual in Oriental
decoration but appropriate to the daintiness of the material.

Agave

Desert-born, dweller of the wilderness, the agave possesses the magnificent beauty that belongs only to enduring strength. Every tourist has seen it in the hot American wastelands; each island of the West Indies has its own variety; Mexico knows it as the maguey. The maguey is as much a part of Mexican life as the pandanus is of Polynesian civilization. Among the more than three hundred species of the agave grown in Mexico and Central America, some produce strong fibers for cord and rope; others furnish a base for soap products; still others provide pulque and mescal, drinks dear to the Mexican palate.

Many of the smaller agaves are cultivated in the southern portions of the United States as specimen plants or, in large gardens, for edging walks and terraces where a sharply definitive growth is desirable. The great clumps of heavy, stiff leaves once established remain for many years. The blades, like those of most desert succulents, are margined and tipped with cruel spines. In some varieties the leaves are gray or green, a few with pale banding of yellow or white; but the usual tone is the blue-green all too infrequent in plant colors. If the heart of the plant is removed and peeled down, sheath by sheath, very interesting abstract designs can be created. The sheathings are creamy-white at first, but with only a brief exposure to the air they become the lovely blue-green of the blades.

Variety after variety, the florescence of the agaves is unmistakably idiosyncratic. Some never flower; others blossom periodically. Best known through art forms is the noblest agave, the century plant, with leaves six feet long. When fifteen or more years old, it grows a stalk twenty-five to forty feet high with flower panicles terminating the high lateral branches. In stately beauty it stands once above the gray desert at its feet; once only, and then dies.

Agave

Agave and Gladiolus

AGAVE

Desert and tropics, Orient and West meet in this extravagantly simple design of agave and torch ginger. Sharply pointed cones of the agave sheaths, contiguous at their base, diverge with a precision wholly consonant with the stiffness of the plant. The mathematical lines of the arrangement are relieved by the spreading shadows on the background and the warm glow of the ginger, whose basal flower is fully open to show the little fat candle in its holder. The container is a bowl of Japanese wormwood with lacquer lining.

Amaryllis

THE TRUE amaryllis, the belladonna lily, is a bulbous plant from South Africa. The term *amaryllis*, however, is applied commonly to all the nearly related plants that resemble the belladonna lily. The amaryllis of the United States is a greenhouse plant except in areas where it encounters only light frost. In the north it makes an attractive window garden; or the pots can be set outside in summer. Wherever it accepts outdoor residence, it is a lusty bloomer of easy culture. It enjoys a sunny location in light, rich soil, well drained. As the blooming period approaches, it needs frequent feedings of liquid manure with liberal irrigation. Because the period of growth is long and the blossoms profuse, the bulb is so exhausted at the end of the season that complete and prolonged rest is essential to restore vitality for the next year.

The various species of amaryllis subjects differ considerably in habits of growth. Most of the older varieties blossom before the leaves appear. The strong stalks push through the ground in early summer, each bearing a several-flowered umbel of lilylike blossoms, usually funnel-shaped and almost always large and showy. The colors range from purest white through delicate pinks to resplendent reds. Many of the newer hybrids have petals of vivid red with heavy stripings of white. The foliage is basal, the strap leaves in many varieties appearing after the flowers are gone. Yet some of the most gorgeous hybrids produce leaf and bloom together; and the flame of the flowers above the rich dark green of the shining leaves is exceedingly beautiful in the garden or in arrangements.

If the amaryllis is picked in the opening-bud stage, it will last four or five days, equally well with or without water. It is adaptable, then, for artificial treatment: as tiebacks on curtains for beautiful parties; or in appliqué effect on mural backgrounds for large banquets.

Amaryllis

Amaryllis and New Zealand Flax

AMARYLLIS

Floral material that can exist dry as easily as when placed in water offers tempting possibilities for artificial manipulation. An old, broken bough, jagged and gnarled, in a container of crackle pottery establishes the principal lines of the arrangement. Massed at the base and perched in those crotches of the tree which indicate the linear pattern are blossoms of hybrid amaryllis in gay defiance of realism. Three amaryllis leaves create a smart contrast to the red and brown tones of the design.

ANTHURIUM

Rich exotic material seems doubly splendid when arranged with artful restraint. Two anthurium spathes against caladium leaves securely base the vertical branch of the African silver tree. The massed leafage of the tree supports the second vertical of the pattern made by the anthurium blades. The slightly turned spathes give the merest suggestion of a curve. Here is contrived simplicity combined with primitive simplicity in the bowl of hand-hewed wood.

Anthurium

THE ANTHURIUM is a perennial from the tropics of South America. More than five hundred species already are catalogued, with new varieties appearing constantly because the species cross easily. Yet of this vast number only a few have been seen in temperate zones, where the known types are widely popular with florists. The culture of the anthurium is extremely difficult for the home gardener since the plant requires a tropical environment which can be created only in a warm greenhouse with an atmosphere of high humidity. The soil must be a loam rough with fibrous content. Fern roots or sphagnum moss can be chopped and added to the earth to provide as much humus as possible, for the anthurium needs a great deal of moisture. The exacting demands of the plant will prevent much attempt at home propagation; yet it is readily available in the commercial market, from both imported and greenhouse sources.

The anthurium is beautifully showy. The kind seen most frequently is popular because of its floral display, which consists of two parts. The large flat spathe, or bract, six inches or more in width and a much elongated heart in general shape, is brilliant in color and texture. Usually red or orange-red, it looks waxen, almost like a thin sheet of lacquered metal. From the head of this spathe rises a spike of densely packed tiny blossoms. These are the true flowers. The leaves are also large and arrow- or heart-shaped with a strongly defined midvein. From the standpoint of beauty anthuriums seem to divide into two groups. In the first, the flower is excitingly lovely; in the other, the flowers are inconspicuous, sometimes even unattractive; but the foliage is large and handsome, velvety in texture.

The anthurium, when fresh, can be kept as long as a month. Dramatic in itself, it should be used alone or with very simple material, preferably something similar in shape, like the caladium or strelitzia leaf.

Anthurium and Strelitzia Leaves

Anthurium and Yucca

Apple

THE APPLE has come to us from a distant time and place. Native of eastern Europe and southwestern Asia, and found in the remains of prehistoric dwellings, it must have been as important in ancient civilizations as it is today. We consider it the essential fruit. It adapts itself to almost any kind of temperate environment, but it does not enjoy long stretches of hot, dry weather. Even irrigation does not compensate entirely for a dry atmosphere without rainfall. If the apple were permitted to choose its earth, probably it would select clay loam. The spreading branches and sturdy leaf growth provide good shade for warm days, and the general appearance of the tree justifies its use as an ornamental; but if space is a determinant, the variety must be selected carefully. Orchard species when full-grown require a very considerable spread, but the dwarf varieties are highly satisfactory for the small home garden.

Growing outside or set within the house, nothing is more typical of late spring than apple blossoms. In delightful contrast to the habits of many flowering fruits, the leaves and the flowers are present together on the branches, and the single blossoms are set usually against a cluster of foliage. The slightly cupped petals are white with the faintest flush of pink; the whole effect is so nearly a glowing translucence that the very word *apple blossom* has come to mean youthful beauty. In the same way the vibrant green of the leaves has given its name to color nomenclature.

The branches are beautiful at any period of their cycle arranged alone in naturalistic effect. Or they may serve as background for spring flowers, preferably those of choice or delicate nature. Because the flowers shatter at a touch, pick in bud stage and immerse the entire branch until crisp. Then it may be set in a shallow container where the buds will swell and open day by day.

APPLE BLOSSOM

Simple material can acquire elegance through highly formal treatment, with its perfection of detail. Spare branches of the apple tree are bent into tranquil curves, interrupted only by short twigs whose irregularity produces essential variation and directs attention to the few scattered blossoms left upon the bough. Interest centers in the peonies, since their coloring resembles the faint blush of the apple blossom. The alabaster container has the same fastidious hue to accord with the sparse lines and scattered material.

Apple Blossom

Apple Blossom and Azalea

Artichoke

THE ARTICHOKE is the aristocrat of the garden patch. Delicious to taste, eccentric in growth, and unique in vegetable beauty, it stands aloof from the common run of market truck. Unlike most foods it matures in winter. Many people never have tasted its buttered succulence, so restricted is its habitat. The globe artichoke comes from southern Europe and northern Africa. It thrives, then, only in limited southern areas of the United States. To be sure, it will exist elsewhere, but it does not produce the good heads of the southern plants; and winter care is tedious and difficult. The most suitable locations are frost-free in winter, cool and foggy in summer. At best the artichoke is temperamental.

The unripened flower bud is the marketable portion of the plant. The edible parts are the soft top of the stem, the fleshy receptacle of the flower, and the part of the scales, or bracts, surrounding the flower bud. Only tender, succulent scales make good food. Inside these bracts, at the base of the cone-shaped flower head, is a pad of fine, prickly hairs commonly called the choke, which never is eaten. This choke is the flower substance. When the bud is fully ripened, the scales have become thin, dry, and hard —completely inedible; but the pad of pale, sharp hairs has risen to the tip of the bud and pushed out into lovely color, the most beautiful of thistle purples. The food of the marketplace has given way to the material of the floral artist.

Angular design suits the brusque beauty of the artichoke. Set the coarse, brown stalks in blunted verticals or sharp diagonals, with the flower heads marking the points. Then the dynamic artistry of the arrangement will be disclosed by the vivid purple tufts. The artichoke is especially good for dry arrangements because the flower retains its color after drying.

Artichoke

Artichoke and Palm Fiber

[3 4]

ARTICHOKE

This study shows how seemingly minor details can work homely material into distinguished compositions. Stalks of cane grass peeled to a layer of succulent brightness relieve the grayness of the artichoke placements. Even the angular slashing of the tops is an interesting finish. Looped grass leaves, so placed that their stripings meet variantly at each juncture, fatten the too-slender placements and balance the artichoke flowers. The container contributes: set horizontally, the splint basket reveals a line pattern of background between the splints.

Aspidistra

ARTISTS in flower arrangement are aware of the great beauty inherent in good foliage material. All too often the leaves natural to the flowers of the arrangement cannot be used. If they grow close to the blossom, they obscure petal detail. Sometimes they appear in bunches or are scraggly, in either event destroying the clean lines of the design. Furthermore, any leaf structure that will become waterlogged when the branch is immersed for conditioning must be removed, since rotting foliage is highly unpleasant. The arranger, then, should make use of supplementary material to provide the necessary greenery for the composition.

Aspidistra, of the lily family, is the first choice for leaves of the broad strap variety. It lives naturally in China and Japan; in the United States it is a house plant except for frostless areas where it grows readily. The leaves are large, fifteen to twenty inches long, narrowing to a sharp point at the tip, and very handsome. The variety most frequently seen is a vivid, glossy green. Another form is variegated with white stripes that disappear if the bulb is set in rich soil. The aspidistra is resistant to conditions that kill many plants. It endures dust, smoke, rough handling, and changing temperatures so easily that it has been called the cast-iron plant. Not the least of its merits is the fact that the leaves will last for months after cutting, a circumstance of considerable interest to anyone who buys his material.

The leaf is popular with florists because of its adaptability. Though tough, it is pliant enough to be manipulated into any desired form. Roll it into shape, tie it in that position, and immerse in water overnight. It will retain the shape it has been given. The aspidistra will combine with any material, but is especially good with flowers of distinction like amaryllis, camellias, or ginger.

ASPIDISTRA

An informal classical Japanese arrangement is the basis for this design. Favorite among the Orientals is the bamboo stalk hollowed to hold water, often employed to indicate varying earth elevations. Aspidistra foliage has been used alone, since the Japanese never combine flowers with this plant; and a few of the leaves have been furled very slightly to suggest careful Oriental manipulation. The abundant material has been set in tight placements with close overlapping to suggest the narrow verticals that the Japanese admire.

Aspidistra and Aralia Leaves

Aspidistra and Kniphofia Blossoms

Aster

Horticulturists have combed the earth for the beautiful things that grow. The great spread of the United States in latitude; the deserts and the seacoasts, the plains and the mountains; the fogs and drought and rain: each of them welcomes some wayfarer from half a world removed. Sometimes one would think America has no flowers of her own, so diligently has she sought the exotic. She has them in plenty, plants of substance and beauty; one of them is the aster. The North American asters are wild flowers, very lovely, of great and diverse tastes: loving sun or seeking shade; reveling in rich soil or living sparsely among the rocks. Most of them bloom in the autumn, winsome flat ray-flowers of white, blue, red, and purple, the flower our great-grandparents used to call the star plant. Hybridizers have done little with the native asters; most of the garden species are wild varieties transplanted and little changed. We call them Michaelmas daisies. European horticulturists, probably in the same search for the remotely beautiful, have developed numbers of named types from American varieties.

The annual we know as the aster providing lavish display of color in autumn gardens is not really an aster at all, though it does claim a remote kinship. It is the Asiatic callistephus, but for all time to come it probably will be called the garden aster. Because it thrives in any good soil, it makes an excellent border plant, with ample choice of petal forms. The single varieties are not so showy as the doubles, but are more delicate in coloring. Among the double blossoms are those with petals curling in toward the center, some with rays tipping back toward the stem, and blooms with quilled edges.

Condition the flowers by removing two thirds of the leaves, then immersing the long stems in deep water. If not arranged alone, they combine attractively with slender, vertical flower forms or foliage.

Aster

Aster and Gladiolus

ASTER

The subtle harmony of the half-tones makes this arrangement satisfying.
Since the asters and the gladioli are almost the same shade of purple, the
deeper tone of the grapes makes more noticeable the pale centers of the
flowers and gives the asters a prominence they would not otherwise have
obtained. The antique lead pitcher was chosen for its color neutrality in
this analogous color scheme.

Bamboo

GRASSES bring rest and comfort to the earth: acres of bluegrass under a summer sun, cool cushion for the feet; tall grasses bending lightly before the wind, the bamboo; and one recalls the feathery giants of the tropics. The true bamboo is an enormous, woody grass grown for ornament and for use. The man of the West knows his fishing pole, but the Oriental uses bamboo in construction of fences, houses, canoe outriggers, vases, musical instruments. In the United States the bamboo, together with the several related forms, functions in ornamental planting. It succeeds best in deep, rich soil heavily irrigated. Set in partial shade, it makes a surprisingly rapid growth, though never reaching the amazing heights of the tropics. Stout varieties form good protective hedge or screen material. For bold effects in a large garden, plant the bamboo in groups; for delicacy place them before evergreens where the light foliage will trace fugitive patterns against the dark background. The Japanese never mass bamboo but let a few stalks create a garden picture, probably the best way to employ them in a small garden.

The Orientals use the bamboo as a living arrangement. To prepare it for the house remove the first dividing layer and fill the top section with water. After drilling holes through the side of the stalk into the lower sections just below the node, fill these sections with water. The stalk will leaf out and this fresh green foliage will remain for months.

The bamboo is not the only ornamental grass. A clump of striped cane will fill an empty corner in the yard. Wild rice or the common reed grass is handsome beside a pool. Taller than wild rice, with equally fine leaves, the reed flowers in beautiful silky plumes.

Grasses create striking arrangements where space and airiness are essential to the design.

Bamboo and Chrysanthemums

Bamboo

[4 3]

BAMBOO

The beauty of very simple things is most apparent in spare treatment. One growing stalk of bamboo with its three airy branches holds sufficient importance for the entire design. The short stalk, barren except for the withered twigs, and the small spray of nandina filling the end of the bamboo tray serve together to balance the main placement. The giraffe is too slender to attract attention to itself; by its position it directs the view to the center of interest.

BANANA

Color is most dramatic in uncluttered arrangements. Here the picturesque
wild mountain banana is displayed rather than the green species commonly
seen. Stalks and sheaths, vividly red, outline the simple pattern. Sharp contrast is supplied by the dark green of the one leaf; but the brilliant red of
the midvein relates the leaf to the color pattern, as do the red mottlings
on the blossom. A cinnabar vase of the same color completes the design.

Banana

THE BANANA, originally from southeastern Asia, is so purely tropical that it has colonized most tropical regions and is solidly established through the Americas. Wherever the banana is produced extensively, it is a valuable food source, usually as vegetable, not fruit. In the United States it is planted only for ornament. Many southern gardens use it as single specimen or in clumps or rows for the beauty of the foliage.

Even in the temperate zones it makes a huge growth, almost treelike. The main stem, so large that it looks like the trunk of a tree, is made of sheathings of the leaf stalks in tight, overlapping layers. The leaves growing from these wrappings are very large and divided down the center by a heavy midrib. Flapped in the tropic winds, the enormous leaves split along the transverse veins until the foliage looks like narrow, ragged pennants hanging from slender spars. The stalk bears only once, then dies; but meantime suckers have grown up around the base which make new plants. The flowering head is very elaborate. Gorgeously colored segments hanging in long, budlike form are bracts. As the cluster matures, these scales lift, one after another, to reveal the small flowers beneath. Then the bracts drop from the stem. On the variety most frequently seen the flower cluster is rich purple and red-violet.

Other ornamental species grow as successful potted plants, or outdoors in southern gardens. One of them, the Abyssinian banana, is very spectacular. It is forty feet tall in its home mountains, with leaves sometimes as much as twenty feet long, centered with a midrib of brilliant red and bearing flower bracts of dark red-brown. The ancient Egyptians used this banana as motif in their sculpture.

To condition, immerse the leaf. Lemon juice applied to the cut edges of the sheath will prevent discoloration.

Banana

Banana and Dieffenbachia Leaves

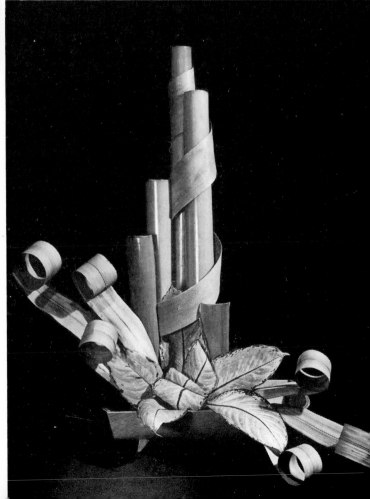

[4 7]

Bells of Ireland

THE GARDENS of long ago sheltered an attractive flower, usually dark red, of peculiar behavior. It opened late in the afternoon except on cloudy days and went back to sleep in the morning. Thus it acquired its popular name of four-o'clock. Today it grows wild in the southern part of the United States through the autumn and into the winter, bright as of old; we know, however, that we admire not a flower but the calyx, or flower-holder. The poinsettia is another plant of innocent masquerade. The flowers form the tiny yellow cluster at the top of the stalk. They pass unnoticed because of the gorgeous bracts that surround them, looking like painted discs upon the long, green leaves. Flowering dogwood, hepatica, and anemone—none have flowers in the ordinary sense.

Except the poinsettia all these plants are old favorites. We are not surprised, then, to see another plant of cherished memory. Under a modern name, the bells of Ireland, given it from its color and form, it grows extensively through the southern areas of the United States. The small rounded or heart-shaped leaves are attractive, but the most interesting feature is the calyx enclosing tiny white flowers. In the shade the calyx is blue-green; in the sun the color fades almost to chartreuse. Originally from Europe, but so long ago that its origin is forgotten, the flower is the Molucca balm or shell flower of our great-grandparents. After defoliation the green cups hang exactly like little green bells, charming in arrangements either alone or in combination. The cut branches need total immersion to strengthen the tip of the stem. During immersion the stalks assume beautiful or weird forms effective in arrangements. Since the plant dries well, holding its form and modifying its color to silver beige, it is good in dried arrangements.

BELLS OF IRELAND

This highly formal arrangement is daring in its combination of materials; the use of unrelated components intrigues the observer to close scrutiny. The bells do not seem to belong with the hydrangeas because of the contrast between their spriggy growth and the massed hydrangea heads with dark foliage. Their importance and congruity are discovered, however, in their fragile echoing of the major line pattern and in the similarity of their bracts to the form of the hydrangea florets.

Bells of Ireland

Bells of Ireland and Pomegranate

Bird's-Nest Fern

Ferns have a cool beauty not found in any other type of plant. For those who love ferns, there is no possible substitute. The hardy species will grow in gardens of the temperate zone if set in suitable locations. They like a good deal of shade; for that reason they can be used to cover difficult spots on the north side of buildings where flowers cannot succeed. If the soil is enriched with leaf mold, and if they are kept damp, they will thrive. Most ferns want their crowns at least partly above ground and sufficient drainage so that the roots do not stand in water; they like moisture, but they are not marsh plants. The United States has so many native ferns that all regions can find a few hardy varieties for garden growth.

The tender fern lives in the greenhouse or in pot culture either as hanging basket on a protected porch or within the house. The bird's-nest fern belongs to this tender division; it is one of the most dependable ferns for interiors. At first glance it does not look like a fern because the fronds are not divided, nor is the margin dentate. It presents a broad, flat, very shiny green leaf sometimes as much as three feet long, shaped like an aspidistra leaf. But there the similarity stops. The new frond is rolled up, as are all fern fronds, with the tip inside. The leaves all emerge from one central point forming at their base a crown clump that resembles a bird's nest. This fern grows wild through Mexico, Central America, south to Brazil, and in the tropics of Asia. As tender ferns go, it is considered reliable, needing little soil when grown in peat.

Ferns combined with woodland plants can create an illusion of forest and stream, of cool mosses and shining rocks wet with trailing grasses.

Bird's-Nest Fern

Bird's-Nest Fern with Day Lilies

BIRD'S-NEST FERN

Plants from a distinctive environment combine felicitously with material from similar surroundings. In a container of wood bark, fronds of the bird's-nest fern are placed to show the natural curl of the leaf. The cymbidium is a happy choice: it is a tree-perching orchid and therefore belongs in this setting; the green of the petals tones with the green of the fern, and the yellow blends with the bark.

Bougainvillea

THE TROPICS have given us our most showy ornamentals. From South America, for the most part from Brazil, comes the bougainvillea, a tall-climbing, woody vine of magnificent color. In its native environment, if left unpruned, the typical form reaches sixty or even one hundred feet; in that same location the plant is used frequently as hedge material and fence cover, subjected to the rigorous pruning necessary to maintain the form. It accommodates itself easily to necessity.

In the United States the bougainvillea is planted where a heavy mat of growth is desired. Like the wistaria it will dress an arbor or pergola, drape a porch, or cover a building. Also, like ivy, it is a successful tree-climber. It develops a sizable trunk that sends up stout, woody stems to great length even in this country. But here, also, it must be trimmed severely to keep it within desirable limits. This extravagance of growth makes it hard to manage in northern greenhouses where its establishment has been attempted. In such latitudes one should follow the example of some florists and treat the vine as a trimmed pot-plant. In milder climates, where it grows outdoors, it is friendly to almost any kind of soil, if it is given full sunlight.

The spectacular beauty of the bougainvillea lies in its bracts. The blossoms themselves are so inconspicuous that many observers never see them. Each tiny tubular flower is surrounded by three large bracts of flamboyant color. The original magenta, the only kind available for many years, is supplemented now by other varieties in crimson, scarlet, rust, and royal purple. Along with these splashing hues comes one quiet vine with bracts of lovely clear white.

To prepare the plant for arrangement remove all the leaves. Then immerse the branch, flowers and all, in water until the bracts are crisply papery. Long cuttings make dramatic silhouette patterns or suitable background material for other flowers.

Bougainvillea

Bougainvillea and Day Lilies

BOUGAINVILLEA

Pagan splendor requires an ornate container and a profusion of brightly colored material. In this design a Caribbean girl wears a handsome head-dress. Blossoms of the bougainvillea, heavily massed, form the base, from which depends one long spray interwoven with oleander to fill the empty spots on the stem. The tall diagonal, which reaches the peak of wild elegance, is made of heavily scented tuberoses. Brilliant rubrum lilies in a sweeping curve unify the design.

BROOM

Slender material is lovely in Oriental design. This arrangement shows the three levels of plant distribution seen in all Japanese floral art except the very early works. From a clustered base the stems spread like natural growth; the broom is so pliant that with slight pressure it assumes and retains these graceful curves. An almost total absence of leaves, and scant floral growth, make broom an ideal choice for this design. The container is a bronze *usubata* from Japan.

Broom

BROOM is a term of clouded meaning. We speak of Scotch broom and Spanish broom; we interchange broom and genista. Scotch broom, the original, belonging to the pea family, was a resident of the Mediterranean native to Europe, Asia, and Africa. The tall, slender plant grows readily in sunny positions in open ground. Not particular as to soil, it prefers a light, sandy loam. For that reason the broom often is set on hillsides and raw, exposed banks, where it succeeds much better than in good soil. It does not transplant readily. Should it freeze, it will grow again from the roots the following year. Despite its lack of foliage—the thin, reedlike branches are almost entirely leafless—the plant is highly ornamental. It makes its best showing in spring and early summer, when the brilliant flowers, in small racemes of true, clear yellow, shine like the sun itself against the bright green stems.

The broom called florist's genista is an evergreen shrub not so tall as the Scotch broom and more bushy, more compact in growth. The leaves are very tiny. Dense clusters of yellow flowers cover the plant in spring and summer, but often are forced into earlier bloom for the Easter trade. This bush is not so hardy as the Scotch broom. While it grows readily in southern areas, farther north it is a greenhouse subject.

Spanish broom is a handsome plant with rushlike stalks resembling the Scotch broom, very little foliage, but showy flowers. The fiber from the stalks is used by the Spanish people in the manufacture of ropes and cords, therefore the popular name of weaver's broom. It grows freely in South America and warm areas of the United States.

Broom is manipulated easily for floral arrangements. Through gentle pressure of the fingers the stem assumes and retains desired positions. If tied in place, it will dry in that shape. The stems need deep immersion.

Broom

Broom and Pansies

Cactus

THE CACTUS is one of the strangest plants in the world, yet among the most interesting. Its entire structure, its every cell, is given over to the one problem of maintaining existence, mere living. Merciless in self-defense, uninviting, even rebuffing an approach, it rewards one who patiently waits at a distance with flowers whose delicate beauty is hard to surpass. The cactus belongs almost entirely to the Western Hemisphere. While more varieties are found in Mexico than in any other one locality, cactus growth extends generously through the southern areas of the United States and many parts of South America. Scattered varieties are found even in British Columbia and Nova Scotia.

Cactus care is not difficult, for the plant needs only three things: dry atmosphere, dry footing, and unlimited fresh air. In its natural location, the desert, most of the very light rainfall occurs at seasons other than winter, when the earth dries very quickly. Rot brings certain death.

The cactus is a plant of varied shape and color. Tree forms, many-branched, have queerly slablike stems. Saguaro, the largest cactus in the world, grows only in one small area of the United States, where it rears its stout arms sometimes sixty feet in the air. Apart from this giant, and the huge barrel cactus, are many small plants, flat, or rounded, or sharply angular. Leaves in the ordinary sense are few or none; stems swollen and shaped much like leaves take their place. The flowers are lovely, brilliant in color and texture.

Cactus makes beautiful permanent arrangements. The very small varieties can be planted in attractive containers in the same dry potting mixture used for succulents. In a light, well-ventilated room they will thrive at room temperature if they are not given too much water. Like African violets they should not be watered from above where the moisture can stand on the crown.

CACTUS

Rugged material should be interpreted with pitiless clarity. Two kinds of cactus have been placed to suggest the close and disordered grouping of desert plants. The blossoms at the base belong to the three growing stalks already in flower, but the manner of placement is concealed by a piece of volcanic rock from Hawaii. The porous surface of the rock suggests the pits on the blade cactus from which the spines emerge. The rough pottery platter is earth-colored.

Cactus

Cactus and Sea Forms

Caladium

Our decorative foliage plants come from the tropics. Like the anthurium, its distant cousin, the caladium is from the hot rain-forests of South America. In the United States it is a warm-greenhouse resident. If one provides difficult but necessary culture, he can grow the hardier varieties outdoors for a brief period of summer. They afford beautiful ground cover for shaded areas or furnish fine divisional markings between the flowers of the north border. Indoors or outdoors the tubers need rich soil, high humidity, and warmth, with feedings of liquid manure every two or three weeks. In autumn, when defoliation begins, irrigation is reduced; for after the last leaf is gone the plant becomes dormant and must be removed from the ground. During the long rest period regulate both temperature and moisture with considerable precision. Despite its beauty, few home gardeners in temperate zones relish the hazards of caladium culture.

The caladium leaf is a large, thin blade shaped much like the anthurium spathe, with the stalk fastened not to the base or the top but to the middle. Thus the leaf slopes obliquely on the plant, a position effective for bedding purposes or flower arrangements. In the hardiest species the foliage is largely green, but in the fancy-leaf caladiums the color patterns are almost unlimited. The basic design comprises a central area bordered by a margin of another but harmonizing hue, perhaps spotted or mottled, and always embellished with highly colored veins: bright-red veins in a white blade; blade pale green at the margin, with an almost transparent disk and veining of red-violet; red blade, green-margined, with venation of dark purple. These spathes of brilliant exotic loveliness wilt in moments unless completely immersed. Condition them, set in a low bowl, then one has brought the tropics within the room.

Caladium

Caladium with Curculigo Capitulata

CALADIUM

This arrangement of caladium leaves with gloxinia blossoms and foliage is simple to execute but luxurious in impression. The spathes are placed to display every aspect of their exotic beauty: the lovely vein pattern on the upper surface, the heavy ribs beneath, the pendulating dips of the margin. Purple gloxinia is beautiful, but it could not have exaggerated the venation of the blades as does this crimson flower. Moss at the bases of both plants suggests the shade of their native environment.

Calla Lily

SOUTH AFRICA is the home of the calla lily, long a favorite of florists and gardeners. In temperate areas it grows permanently in the garden as a small, low ornamental attaining full growth and perfection of beauty in partial shade. For that reason, if planted in rows, as so often it is placed, it should be given some protection by fence or house. A more sightly use of the calla is to mass the plants in small groups. Given all the water and the manure that it needs, it develops a luxuriant richness of foliage that is extremely decorative.

The leaves are basal, borne on heavy stalks and shaped much like a greatly elongated and broad-based arrowhead sharply pointed at the tip. Those of the common calla are smooth and deeply green with outer edges often curled loosely toward the under side. Other varieties display a variegated foliage. The green of the leaf is usually not so lustrous as that of the common calla but is made interesting by its pattern of dark and light, where the broad surface is shot with flecks or dots of white or cream or palest yellow.

The flowers are even more beautiful than the leaves. The spathe is a rich cream, narrow and deeply cupped at the base, flaring outward in broad, sweeping lines to a narrowed tip that recurves sharply down or even backward toward the stalk. The spadix, covered with tiny flowers crowded close on the narrow, rounded shaft, reaches slightly above the mouth of the trumpet formed by the curling edges of the spathe. There are other varieties, pink or yellow, but none can equal the severe beauty of the common calla. Perhaps the most dignified of our flowers, it is best arranged alone or with its own foliage. Without total immersion the leaves wilt in the arrangement. The flower stays fresh in a shallow container without conditioning; therefore treat only the leaves.

Calla

Calla and Aspidistra

CALLA LILY

Artlessness depends upon a carefully gauged precision. Blades of New Zealand flax used at the base are carefully graded in length and angle of direction to fall short of complete symmetry by the merest trifle. The vertical placement of variegated aspidistra rises first on the left, then on the right. The exquisite spiral of the callas not only traces a curve, but in so doing the lilies are rotated on a central axis to describe a half turn. The transition between the strong spikes and the softened lilies is accomplished by the folded blades of the aspidistra at the base.

Camellia

To PROPAGATE handsome camellias was once the test of home gardening. Because the culture of the plant was not generally understood, the enterprise was a considerable floricultural hazard to the untried amateur. Today we know that the camellia, like many another Asian, is happy in American earth, maturing successfully in good soil kept loosely well-drained and conditioned with much fertilizer. The camellia grows slowly, but a manure mulch to keep the roots moist will stimulate hardy development. Shrubs in half-shaded locations produce the best floral display. The plant itself will live in the open; it is the flowers that resist sunlight. Both singles and doubles, ranging from white through the pinks to dark red, are short-stemmed, close to the branch.

Although the camellia is raised chiefly for the blossoms, the entire plant is handsome. The leaves sit neatly upon their stems, vividly green with a shining luster unique in many gardens. The slow growth of the plant impels many gardeners to pick the almost stemless flower rather than to cut a branch. The only possibility, then, for floral design is to float the blossom or to wire it artificially in brief, unnatural display. This limited use cannot reveal its true beauty, since the bloom grows against a background of its foliage, one flower and three to five leaves forming a unit on the shrub. To arrange the entire branch as the Orientals do is to exhibit the real loveliness of the camellia. Choose two good varieties for cutting. Plant several specimens of both kinds, enough to rotate their use, cutting each bush only in alternate years and thus permitting it to recover its growth. To ensure lasting qualities, one habitually picks flowers in the opening-bud stage. The camellia is one of the few exceptions to this recognized principle. If the blossom is partly open, with the outer petals slightly cupped, it will outlast both buds and fully opened blooms.

Camellia

Camellia and Heather

CAMELLIA

This arrangement is planned to show how camellias can be used eco-
nomically with a sparing need for their own foliage. The central feature
is the three camellias set against their own foliage. Sprays of lilies of the
valley with their leaves build this main placement to suitable proportions.
Then folded leaves of the canna, together with cannas in slender furls,
provide adequate background. Two canna leaves, one open and one furled,
drape the formal alabaster vase.

Canna

THE TRAIL of the canna winds through the tropics. From Malaysia and the Philippines north into China, around the Caribbean in the West Indies and on the mainland, down both sides of South America one finds these remote cousins of the banana. Europe made fine use of them in the second half of the nineteenth century. The horticulturists of the continent had developed new strains from the tropical originals. Most of them were tall and very leggy, with small flowers not too interesting in color. Since they were grown largely for their foliage, the weak floral display was no great disadvantage. In England they were grouped in large plantings in parks and public places until people grew weary of them and they fell into disfavor. Of recent years innumerable crossings by skilled hybridizers have produced extremely beautiful, stately plants bearing large and very showy flowers, yet still retaining their vigorous foliage.

If the earth is to its liking, the canna will grow easily. It needs a soil richer than is required by many plants, thorough irrigation during the summer, and heat. It cannot, therefore, be planted early, nor will it last beyond the chill of autumn. The most successful use of the canna is in mass effects. The older planting in geometrically formal beds is still successful for large gardens. In smaller areas it makes beautiful hedges or border planting against large shrubs or trees. It cannot be scattered without plan because the pronounced individuality of its coloring is not tolerant of flowering neighbors.

The shortness of the blooming period urges a considered use in arrangements. Pick the canna in bud; then immerse the entire stalk in water to prolong the life of the flower. The foliage will outlast the bloom by many days; fortunately so, because among blade-leaved plants the canna combines most easily with other flowers. Both the green and the deep redbrown suggest the lushness of tropic growth.

Canna

CANNA

A small amount of brilliant color can balance a much larger area of either high or low saturation. Folded canna leaves in neat overlappings build a strong background, interesting in its pattern of diagonals with their pointed tips. But the glowing color supplied by the few canna blossoms provides the main interest for the arrangement. The container, a tray of split bamboo finished with a copper lining, sits on a bamboo mat.

CARNATION

The significance of this monochromatic arrangement rests in its richness, both in color and in texture. The tall central placement of ti leaves supplies the darkest tone of the design, a red that is broken only by the veining on the blades. Each rose carnation rests on a cushion of cockscomb celosia whose convoluted folds have the softness of plush. The container is pottery, deep wine with a silvered base.

Carnation

Over two thousand years ago our common garden pink grew in the beautiful gardens of the Greeks; that long ago it was named. Was it the shape of the flower that Theophrastus found very lovely? The Greeks excelled in pure design. Did the color impress him? The original carnation was flesh-colored, and the Greek ideal of beauty was founded on moderation and restraint. Or did he savor the fragrance, the titillating spiciness of cloves? Whatever his reason, he named it the divine flower, the dianthus. Eighteen centuries later, when the forthright Tudors sat the throne, Europeans discovered the beauty of the carnation; gardeners of the flower-minded countries developed each his own idea of floral beauty until by Shakespeare's time the varieties of carnation were legion. So much had been done that it remained for the United States only to perfect what had been established. Using a French strain, American growers developed the perpetual-flowering carnation. In the United States the plant is a hardy perennial in areas having mild winters. Where the summers are very hot or the winters sharply cold, it succeeds best as a greenhouse plant.

Satisfied with the form of the blossom, hybridizers work now to modify the color. Beautiful clear values of solid color are supplemented by blossoms with striped or flecked petals, or petals delicately margined in harmonizing tone. Gardeners of recent years are making attractive use of the single dianthus that is often called the garden pink. More hardy than the florist's carnation, and much more fragrant, the little plant makes a fine edging for the border. The small, short-stemmed flowers grow from dense mats of foliage. Many kinds have beautifully marked petals with fringed edges.

All forms of the dianthus make charming arrangements. The carnation has an unfortunate tendency to fold up or shrivel after it has been arranged. When that happens, recut the stem and immerse up to its head in water. When conditioned, replace in the container.

Carnation

Carnation and Pittosporum

Castor Bean

THE CASTOR bean is so old that its beginnings are lost in antiquity. Probably it is a native of Africa, but before history began it had spread to all parts of the ancient world. Professor Bailey reasoned from its Hebrew name that the Old Testament may have had reference to this plant as the gourd which grew in one night to shelter the disconsolate Jonah and perished as suddenly when attacked by a worm.

Extraordinarily rapid growth is a characteristic of the plant, a considerable asset if one uses it as screen material. In areas of even light frost new plants must be started each year; for all practical purposes, therefore, the castor bean is a tender annual. It is handsome. In the United States it reaches a height of ten feet, as against the forty feet of the tropics. Borne on stalks of rich red, the leaves are large and many-lobed, with toothed edges. New growth is red-bronze, changing as it matures to green, purple-red, or blackish-purple, metallic red, or red with a soft gray bloom—all of them rich, shining colors. The flowers, usually scarlet, cluster tightly in small racemes that stand stiffly erect on short stems and later form blue-green or red-brown seed capsules covered with soft, blunt spines. Seeds, three to a capsule, are smooth and vividly mottled. These seeds supply the world with castor oil.

The castor bean has been considered a garden pest for so long that it is difficult to change popular attitude. Yet no shrub so surely and so swiftly can transform a bare or ugly spot to a corner of tropical beauty. No plant, furthermore, lends itself more easily to floral design since all portions of the plant are decorative. Before arranging, immerse the plant parts in water until stiff, cutting the leaves from the stalk if they are to be used alone. With water treatment the arrangement lasts.

CASTOR BEAN

By indirection the lavish growth of the castor bean is suggested. Many stalks—some large and mature, others slender and young—rise from close grouping to varying heights. Only a few young leaves left on the stalks interrupt the bareness of the vertical stems; but at the base the radiating leaves, fully developed, provide an adequate support for the height. A splendid color contrast between leaves and stems is a leading item of interest.

Castor Bean

Celosia: Cockscomb

Two or three generations ago, when small country fairs were leading social enterprise, a blue-ribboned entry was a rural housewife's ultimate glory. Among the exhibits was a row of flowerpots, each containing a diminutive plant surmounted by one enormous mass of color weirdly turned and twisted in convoluted folds. This was a cockscomb. The sole object of the grower had been to outrage nature, for the prize went to whoever most successfully outwitted the plant and by horticultural blandishment produced the largest bloom on the tiniest growth.

Even in normal conditions the celosia is a peculiar flower. Its home-folks in the tropics of Asia and Africa look upon it more as weed than garden ornament. The United States has elevated it to the level of tropical exotic; for we enjoy the rich colors, we delight in the fantastic shapes. The crested celosia is small, twelve to eighteen inches high, with smooth oval leaves. The single flowers are very tiny, each by itself completely insignificant; through manner of growth they become startlingly showy. Crowded tightly in dense panicles, sometimes wider than the height of the plant, they form spikes of weirdly eccentric shapes: odd balls of twisted fluff, flattened ridges like the bizarre headdress of some caricaturist's rooster—contours that are queerly stiff. Hard and strange the design may be, but the material is soft and velvety. From its shape this crested celosia takes the common name of cockscomb; from its texture it is known as Chinese woolflower. The colors are gorgeous: creamy white, pure red and crimson, purple and violet, purplish pink and yellow.

The cockscomb is better suited to stylistic than to natural design. Choose a container that will exaggerate the color of the flower. Use the celosia alone or with simple material of straight lines and restrained color. It is one of the few plants to dry in natural color. Hang it upside down during the drying process to preserve the form.

Celosia: Cockscomb

Celosia and Larkspur

CELOSIA: COCKSCOMB

The elegance of this arrangement was determined by the container of elaborate dusky bronze. Clusters of red cockscomb rest at the foot and rise in their inevitable folds, supported by magnolia leaves that have been dyed black. An opulent composition justifies the employment of artificial treatments. Red grapes were chosen for their color. The upper cluster unifies the design by bridging the distance between the two portions of the pattern.

Celosia: Plume

THE PLUME celosia is a much larger plant than the crested variety, usually two or three feet tall. It has none of the stiff formality of the cockscomb. The flower spikes have the same dense growth of minute blossoms seen in the crests, but the long racemes stand loosely in simple, straight lines. Moving lightly with the wind, they look like soft, feathery plumes. The color range is wider than in the crested type: ivory, yellow to amber, yellow-red to red-violet, chartreuse and lime green.

All celosias are easy to grow. They should be set in light, rich soil where they will receive full sunlight but still can be kept damp. True to their tropical ancestry, they love moisture; and if their roots are allowed to dry out they lose their leaves. In large landscapes where definite areas of bright color are needed they mass effectively. The texture of the flowers helps in this respect; the bright chenille tufts glow in the sunlight until their brilliance seems to burn the air about them. Some varieties have variegated leaves. Though their spikes are not usually so dense as those of the plain-leaf type, the color of the foliage accentuates the mass effect of the planting.

A distant relative of the celosias and, like them, a member of the amaranth family long has been a popular garden annual. Called sometimes tassel flower or love-lies-bleeding, it exhibits the same long spikes of tiny flowers in chenille texture. The racemes are much more slender than those of the celosia and pendent rather than erect. Some varieties have brilliant foliage, almost blood-red, with green or yellow flower spikes. Others display green leaves with red flowers; but none are so showy as the celosia.

To prepare the celosia for arrangement, remove two thirds of the leaves. Then place the stems in deep water.

CELOSIA: PLUME

The richness of this design comes through accretion. The tall spire and the lower diagonal have been assembled with great care by deftly placing many small stems of the plume celosia to look like one great stalk. The central group unifying the placements differs from the others only that the massing is done in swirling lines. The darkest tones are placed in the center to enrich their tone value. This deepening is especially noticeable where the celosia meets the heavy brown of the iron container.

Celosia: Plume and Pampas

Celosia and Chrysanthemums

Chard

Swiss chard is a beet that renounced the traditional earthy behavior of its family for a wayward life in fresh air. It has no fleshy rootstock like that of the turnip, the beet, or the carrot. Such root as it produces is small and woody, completely inedible. It devotes its abundant vitality to the growth of foliage. Cooked like any other table green, it is more tasty than spinach but not so strongly flavored as beet or turnip tops. A new variety has the same large green leaves as the more common kind, but the stalks and veins are white. Some cooks use only the thick, white stalks of this latter variety, treating them much like asparagus. Chard is planted for food more extensively in Europe than in the United States. It grows quickly, producing a luxuriant leafage that is cut stalk by stalk as needed; a constant succession of new leaves appears to replace those which have been used. If the root is healthy, it will bear until freezing weather.

Even the most ordinary chard is handsome. The bright green foliage, much larger than beet leaves, has thick, heavy veins so firmly placed that the blade substance crinkles and puckers and puffs between the ribs. The edge is exceptionally attractive. Since no portion of the leaf lies flat, the margin flirts out in whimsical undulations to rim the erratic smocking of the blades. This irregularity breaks the glossy surface into hundreds of tiny curves and angles, lustrous in every glint of light. A few varieties have high-colored foliage. One handsome chard is a dark-red and green combination with cherry stalk and veins, a coloring that gives it the trade name of rhubarb chard. The green chards go under several popular names: sea-kale beet, leaf beet, or silver beet. For use in arrangements immerse completely. Chard makes splendid designs either alone or in vegetable or fruit combinations.

Chard

Chard and Dahlias

CHARD

Trying to glamorize the commonplace is futile when the commonplace happens to be so beautiful that it need only be shown to be admired. Red chard, chosen for its color, forms the main placements. The crinkled leaves are supported by slashed lengths of stem which parallel or prolong the main vein. Because the red gladioli are the same color as the veins, they emphasize the chard rather than drawing attention to themselves.

Chrysanthemum: Ball

I

N THE temperate and subtropical regions of the Old World the chrysan-themum was cultivated in the ages before records began. India, Korea, Japan, and China have developed its form and cherished its beauty until it has become symbolic of Oriental art. When the plant first appeared in America, no one can say; in early colonial days, no doubt, since a display of the flowering plants was held by a horticultural society around 1825. Of the thousands of varieties presented by hybridizers, few have remained in cultivation. Probably only seventy or eighty are grown widely, but these are so generally popular that no autumn garden is complete without at least a few plants.

The chrysanthemum needs a light, rich, well-drained soil with ample feeding of fertilizer and liberal water supply. The plant is shrubby, slightly woody; and if it is to develop the bushiness that the ordinary gardener wants for heavy flower production it must be encouraged to grow rapidly. Use liquid manure until the buds set. If garden space permits, chrysan-themums should be planted by themselves. They do not combine attractively with other flowers usually blooming at the same time, nor with all others of their own kind. A chrysanthemum border can be very beautiful if the varieties are chosen carefully for color harmony. Except for true blue and true purple, all hues are represented, from white and pastels through the heavy tones to dark orange, bronze, and red. But the colors are individualistic and definite, as the odor is characteristic and strong; and a careless assortment can be highly disturbing.

A small garden can supply enough flowers for the home since, if one does not disbud the plants to ensure excessively large flowers, they will produce heavily. The stems require conditioning before arrangement, and the flowers are long-lasting. They arrange beautifully in the Oriental manner, supplying ideal ornamentation for a room decorated with Oriental accessories.

Chrysanthemum: Ball

Chrysanthemum and Cattails

CHRYSANTHEMUM: BALL

Repetition is the basis of this design. The ball form of the chrysanthemums is suggested in the grouping of the flowers in incomplete circles. Just as the shape of the mat behind the flowers repeats the circular form of the chrysanthemums, so the delicacy of the woven pattern where every fiber is perceptible is echoed in the prominent veining of the Dieffenbachia leaves. The mat was made in China, and the chrysanthemums are of Chinese origin.

CHRYSANTHEMUM: QUILL

In floral composition design frequently is more important than medium. For sheer beauty the materials themselves are less significant than the manner of their combining. The quill chrysanthemums are attractive but in no way remarkable. The long sweep of the very simple francoa sprays in ascending repetition, the two short branches deftly curved until the chrysanthemums virtually are framed by the francoa, these are the details that create a pattern worthy of the Sèvres bowl.

Chrysanthemum: Quill

THE CHIEF effort of hybridizers today is to increase the length of the chrysanthemum's flowering period. Early varieties begin about September; the late ones last until December, with an extension of a month at each end for a few species. As with the dahlia, the possibilities of form have been almost exhausted. The very tall kinds, sometimes as much as four feet high with many branches and smooth-petaled blossoms, are the Chinese chrysanthemums. The Japanese types bear very large flowers with involved petal arrangement, some of them twisted or curled or loosely set even to shagginess. Most of the single forms are from Korean stock. Usually low-growing, around two feet, and heavy producers, they afford fine garden display and fashion into beautiful arrangements. The pompons are Indian. Within these types are the flower shapes popularly known as spider, plume, feather, quill, hairy, curved—through a long list of descriptive terms.

The huge beauties known as the florist's chrysanthemum are often hardy, but to equal the specimens on the market is a difficult task for home gardeners. In many areas of the United States blossoms of this size and perfection are produced only under glass and with constant care the year around. The home grower needs a plant with a strong root system to carry over to the following year. The pompons are more hardy than other varieties. Even in northern areas they will winter successfully outdoors, for they are as frost-resistant as any garden flower. If one can give little care to his garden, then the pompon by all means should be his choice. Often after all other flowers have stopped blooming, the pompon chrysanthemum still shows bright color. Since the blossoms are small, in the button chrysanthemums even tiny, they must be planted in groups to produce a color effect in the garden.

Chrysanthemum: Quill

Chrysanthemum and Pampas

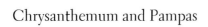

Coral Tree

ONE always notices brilliant color. Even in this flashing generation unusual tones or subtle variations of familiar hues compel attention. When to color is added an engaging form, one wishes to turn against the light, to touch. No one could confront a full-flowered coral tree with unconcern, for few trees in temperate zones are so entirely exotic as this sprightly beauty. The coral tree inhabits warm areas the earth around. Of the fifty or more species some are high shrubs; a few are tall and woody trees. Plantations in South America and the West Indies use the coral tree to shade their coffee and cacao growths. In the United States, where it is merely decorative, it provides gay adornment wherever used. The kind grown most generally in the South is a bushy shrub that sends up new branches each spring. After the foliage has leafed out, umbrella-fashion, the flowers appear in heavy terminal clusters to provide a month of painted glory. Colored a heavily saturate scarlet, they resemble somewhat the beak of a macaw. They look crisply plastic above the bright green leaves—but not gaudy; they are much too rich, too dark for that. Not even in full sunlight do they seem garish. When one touches the flower with the lightest of fingertips, the first notion of rigidly plastic structure shrinks to bare fancy, and the flower becomes softly alive.

A cousin of the same pea family as the coral tree is crotalaria, with its racemes of blossoms, some yellow-green, others yellow with purple streaks. From the shape of the flower the shrub often is called the canary bird tree; from its noisy seed pods, rattlebox.

The graceful, arching branches of these trees fashion easily into soft, flowing lines and to circular design. The attractive foliage is useful in arrangement; but if the contour of the flower is featured, then the branches should be defoliated.

CORAL TREE

Tall sprays of the coral tree, increasing in height as they diverge slightly from their position in the holder, are given stability by the strong leaves of the castor bean. The narrow, deeply slashed lobes continue the suggestion of radiating lines, while the color is but deeper tones of the reds and the greens of the coral tree. Two open blossoms and one bud of epiphyllum provide effective accent, their waxen petals as crisp as the plastic semblance of the coral blossoms.

Coral Tree

Coral Tree and Aspidistra Leaves

Crape Myrtle

A TREE can establish the tone of a landscape. Its height, above even tall shrubs, makes it the most conspicuous feature of the planting; and the spread of its branches decorates a wide area. It will live for the lifetime of the garden, but once lost it cannot soon be replaced. A flowering tree, then, must be chosen with more care than a shrub, for it will be a constant companion through all the years to come. The moments of perplexity that attend our search for the perfect tree are occasioned not from any dearth of material; it is, rather, the plenteousness of beauty that confuses us.

Manifestly desirable among handsome flowering trees is the crape myrtle, which has traveled half the world to reach our gardens. Probably it originated in China, though it thrives with enough ease and profusion in India to be native to that land. In the United States it lives throughout the southern areas. Without specific soil requirements, needing no particular care, it persists even through neglect. Standing in forgotten parkways or fronting the full sun on raw hills, it thrives in beautiful unconcern of human remissness. Since it can be kept low, from eight to ten feet, it is useful for hedges or backgrounds. If unpruned, it quickly reaches its full height of twenty to thirty-five feet. The matured tree has a long blooming season; the several species flower from June to October. Growing in bunches at the ends of the branches, the blossoms resemble little tufts of crepe paper. The petals are crinkled or fringed, with numbers of long, curved stamens. The variety grown for years in old gardens is bright pink, but other colors are not uncommon. White, the palest rose flush, and purple are well established. Branches of the tree make charming arrangements. When first cut they wilt easily, but a long, deep immersion after defoliation will crisp the flowers to their original condition.

Crape Myrtle

Crape Myrtle and Palm

CRAPE MYRTLE

Two informal placements of crape myrtle which establish the diverging
pattern of this arrangement are unified by a central spray of rubrum lilies.
The erect ti leaf provides a height proportional to the spread of the crape
myrtle, and the folded leaf makes the transition between the vertical line
and the material at its base. To emphasize the vivid yet refined color of
the design, an antique glass compote has been used as a container.

Crinum

THE CRINUM is a showy plant of unusual beauty related to the amaryllis. Superficially the flowers of the two plants are much alike, except that the crinum trumpet is longer than the amaryllis flower. In other respects the plants differ. The bulb of the crinum is enormous, in some varieties measuring as much as two or three feet; and sometimes it is a huge onion with a neck like a gigantic leek. The plant is too large to be grown commercially. For the same reason it is unsuited to greenhouse culture. The crinum, in consequence, is not cultivated extensively in the United States, though hardy varieties grow freely in southern areas. All crinums need a rich, moist soil with considerable fertilization. In large landscapes against a background of rich, high shrubbery they are indeed lovely.

The leaves are thick and fleshy straps several feet long and stalkless, remaining at least partially green after the flowers appear. The flower stem pushes out between the leaves at the side of the bulb neck; from its sheath day by day the trumpets slowly open.

When plants undergo an extensive natural hybridization that results in many similar species, identification is not easy. A few crinums are established fairly well by name. One magnificent specimen, the Great Mogul of Barbadoes, is a Goliath of lilies. The flower stalk is an inch through and four feet high, so heavy it must be staked. It is topped by an umbel of blossoms, magenta on the outside of the bud, delicate pink inside. The flowers of the milk-and-wine lily are white inside the trumpets, dark red outside. Not all crinums have trumpets. The segments of the swamp lily are so long and narrow that the creamy white blossom resembles a huge star.

The crinum arranges like any lily. Use very shallow water in the container, because the pithy stem disintegrates at the end if the water is deep.

Crinum

Crinum and Cabbage

CRINUM

This profuse arrangement of summer-blooming flowers is characterized by the elegance that belongs to formal design. The blossoms were chosen for the delicacy of their tonal blend. Broad horizontal and vertical lines are made with pink and lavender gladiolus. The important low center is filled with a massing of pink crinum trumpets relieved with a few sprays of tuberoses. Lastly, pink asters in opposing diagonals link the several placements of the dainty harmony.

CYCLAMEN

This arrangement is an interesting study in proportion. The dominant branch of stock was selected for the unusual bending of its stem, a curve that suggested an appropriate pattern. Close clustering of the florets gives sufficient substance to stand as the only vertical placement and support for the figurine. A spaced disposition of the open cyclamen flowers widens the base to a stable foundation for the heavy stock. The two slender buds direct attention to the Madonna.

Cyclamen

SOUTHERN Europe's gift to the florist is the cyclamen. From the Mediterranean north into central Europe it grows wild. In the old days before the soil was taken over for cities and highways and vast industrial enterprises, grassy fields swept the earth for endless miles peopled with the bright things of the plant world. Here the cyclamens dimpled the grass, pointing the way to their tubers, which wild pigs devoured with relish. Perhaps the flower has scaled a figurative precipice, from a feast before swine to the Christmas display of the florist. Whoever receives a cyclamen as gift hopes day by day that it will survive a bit longer, that it will put out one more bloom. For it is a very lovely flower. The heart-shaped leaves rise on short stalks in a heavy cluster, their edges thinly scalloped, the blades variegated with white marbling. The blossoms are white or some shade of rose, with purple or red at the mouth and the segments reflexed completely. The florist's cyclamen is a greenhouse plant. Other much smaller kinds are hardy enough for the rock garden, but few of these forms are known in the United States.

Another gift plant restricted to the house is the gloxinia. Although in South America there are varieties of gloxinia that are garden flowers, the only species cultivated in the United States is from the hot rain-forests of Brazil. Even more showy than the cyclamen, the gloxinia has a long range of colors: white, and white with faintly tinged edges; all kinds of pink and crimson; blue and purple to the richest tones. Often the deep throat of the bell is darker than the flare. The foliage is soft and velvety; the leaves are heavily veined.

Though neither of these plants makes long-lasting cut flowers, total immersion of leaf and flower will preserve their beauty satisfactorily for an arrangement.

Cyclamen

Cyclamen with Tree Branch

Cymbidium

THE ARISTOCRAT of the plant world is the orchid. It lives in privileged seclusion in the greenhouses of fanciers and the homes of gardeners possessed of the knowledge and the time to provide the culture without which the orchid cannot exist. Though most orchids have been found in tropical and subtropical areas, they are known to be widely distributed, living naturally in almost every portion of the earth except regions of extreme dry heat or cold. Florists' displays have acquainted us with the cattleya, the most showy of all orchids. Its magnificent blossoms, remarkable for both size and exquisite color, were long considered most precious for decoration, either in corsage or general design. Popular interest in the orchid has stimulated search and hybridization until now hundreds of varieties are available, many of them more suitable for personal adornment than the splendid cattleya.

The cymbidium is one of the best exotic orchids for home growth. In the high mountains of Asia it is an epiphytic, or tree-perching, plant; not a parasite, but a tenant upon the moss or bark of the limb, drawing its nourishment from the air and the decayed material that accumulates at its roots. The varieties in cultivation are terrestrial orchids attractive at all seasons. The leaves are very green, narrow and sharp, sometimes two feet long. The flowers stand on short, curved stems on a long stalk, the entire raceme arching away from the leaves in a sweeping curve. The floral growth is very persistent; often it lasts for weeks. Since as many as twenty blooms appear on a stem, the cymbidium is one of the most decorative of orchids. The colors are varied: lovely ivory-white tinged with rose or striped with a yellow rib through the center, greenish yellow marked with brown or streaked with violet, dull purple spotted with red. Any cymbidium is beautiful, and it is especially satisfactory in arrangements, because of its lasting qualities.

CYMBIDIUM

A broken tree-fragment shaped like a stump is an ideal support for the cymbidium orchids. The long spray with its many flowers is so placed that the orchids perch upon the tree as if in their natural location. The green leaves are the foliage of the cymbidium. They furnish a tone accent to the arrangement, which otherwise has a very short range of hues.

Cymbidium

Cymbidium and Bird's-Nest Fern

Cypripedium

ALTHOUGH orchids differ in general appearance—in size, shape, and coloring—until they seem unrelated, they have similar plant parts. Always the thick, fleshy roots look almost bulbous; invariably the stems terminate each year's growth with a thickened knob or node called a pseudobulb, which functions as food reservoir. Flowers, unlike those of any other family, are irregular in shape, with only two of the three petals alike. The third petal is lip-shaped; it may be fringed or spurred, or it may loop back upon itself to form a sac.

The cypripedium belongs to the last type, where the enlarged third petal looks like a pouch dependent from the face of the flower. This pouch gives the flower its name. It is known botanically as cypripedium, which translates roughly into "the shoe of Venus"; the common name is lady's-slipper. The plant is hardy in the United States, where in many areas it may be grown in the ground in a cool, moist place. The species indigenous to the United States have been picked ruthlessly until the flower is seen much more frequently in cultivation than it can be found in its native locations, though the climatic conditions are ideally suited to it. The leaves are very handsome, long, beautifully ribbed in fine, narrow corrugations, and rimmed with a knife edge that cuts like paper. The midvein, prominent on the back, shows a delicate white channel on the upper surface. Only a few fragile blossoms appear on the flower stalk. In the moccasin flower the pouch is either pink or white against petals of yellowish green. The yellow lady's-slipper is brilliant but small, the two petals almost greenish, the lip golden yellow. Perhaps most showy is the queen's lady-slipper, with white petals and a large pouch of pale magenta. Whoever owns orchids has material for exquisite arrangements in naturalistic design.

Cypripedium

Cypripedium with Tree Bark

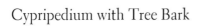

CYPRIPEDIUM

Beautifully ribbed leaves of the wild ground-orchid are precisely placed for pictorial effect. Were they vertical, the design would be stiff enough to destroy the grace of the delicate cypripedium orchids. If they tipped even the least bit farther, they would appear unstable and therefore disturbing. The other leaf placement, a short opposing diagonal, provides a natural position for the flower. The container is a chunk of lava, its porous holes enlarged to insert a small container.

Daffodil

THE NARCISSUS is one of the oldest cultivated flowers. Just where and when it began is uncertain, for it grows natively over a wide spread of the earth, from central Europe to the Mediterranean and on through Asia. The type names within this group are vague and confused. Though narcissus is the general term meant to cover all the species, it is applied popularly to the very fragrant flowers growing in clusters. The daffodil is the blossom with strap leaves whose trumpet is at least as long as the petals. The jonquil originally was one variety only, having clusters of little yellow flowers and round leaves much like small rushes. With extensive culture the plants have been hybridized until these distinctions no longer are clearcut.

But whatever one calls them, the dainty blossoms deserve our affection. They look their best when naturalized. Growing freely in clumps or long drifts as if wild, with some cover vegetation to conceal the unkempt foliage after the period of bloom is over, they make a lovely spring display. If planted in formal beds, they are beautiful when in early green leaf or full flower; but in such planting the late period after the blossoms have died is difficult to manage. For the foliage must be left until it has died down, else the bulbs are not strengthened for the growth of the next year.

The long-trumpet yellow daffodils now are available in many shades of yellow, some with fringed corona or edges slightly crimped, others that are double. The poet's narcissus is an old favorite partly because of its delicate fragrance. The leaves are slender and about eighteen inches long; the white corolla centers in a shallow tube more like a raised ring than a cup with bright red margin. Some of the new daffodils are entirely creamy, almost white.

Daffodil

Daffodil and Palm

DAFFODIL

In this unusual formal arrangement the light-colored flowers at the base establish a small triangle, the design that is completely worked out by the heavy, dark placements. Long stalks of rich hybrid delphinium in lavender, blue, and purple form the dark pattern. For contrast, the yellow grouping was made by using long-stemmed flowers and successively shortening the stems. Tulips and Dutch iris and orchid stock supplement the principal detail of yellow daffodils.

Dahlia

THE DAHLIA is truly pan-American. The parent stock of all garden dahlias in the United States came from the uplands of Mexico; other interesting species grow wild in Central America and northern sections of South America. Origins usually are interesting. When one roams vagrant trails crisscrossing the isthmus between history and legend, he discovers many rare stories. Such was the narrative about a court physician to Philip of Spain in the mighty days when the Spaniards ruled the New World. Sent to investigate the natural life of the strange land, he found in the mountains of Mexico a lovely flower, a primal dahlia. Two hundred years later—here one is on the firm road of history—plants and seeds were sent from Mexico to Europe for study, and the dahlia began the career that has made it one of the most popular flowers in the United States.

Recent developments have proceeded toward two different ends: the perfection of large-flowered varieties for exhibition and the production of small, low types for border planting and home arrangement. We have, as a result, all colors except blue, together with an unlimited choice of flower forms: singles and doubles; flat rays and round, puffy balls; narrow, pointed petals, quilled petals, petals that curve up or turn down.

Highly important in dahlia cultivation is the control of irrigation. Though the plants need much water during the blooming period, they cannot endure soggy earth. To ensure good drainage, therefore, some fanciers prefer sloping ground exposed to considerable sun, at least half the day in full sunlight.

New methods of conditioning dahlias for arrangements have replaced the burning of stems. Since the leaves draw too heavily of the moisture in the container, completely defoliate the stem, then immerse to the neck of the flower, not wetting the petals, and the water will go directly to the blossom.

Dahlia

DAHLIA

Flowers of late summer can express all the ripeness of autumn. A container of brown alabaster establishes the tone. The main placement of tawny dahlias, carefully graded in size to emphasize the one large flower at the center, is supplemented by orange cannas and small plumes of yellow celosia. Sprays of pyracantha give the height necessary to complement the heaviness of the center placement; their slenderness emphasizes the importance of the dahlias.

Daisy

ONG ago in the morning of England someone with the vision of an artist and the words of a poet looked at the grass about his feet, at the low-growing flowers, mere dots of pink and white among the green. Eye of the morning! Eye of day! Day's eye! That little flower is the English daisy. Because it needs cool soil and moist atmosphere, it succeeds better at home than in the United States. In low borders and springtime edgings the daisy makes a particularly fresh and crisp line.

Though the United States has no daisy, we bestow the name recklessly on almost any ray flower new to our markets. The Shasta daisy, to consider it first, is a chrysanthemum developed by Luther Burbank from a native of the Pyrenees. The finely cut, sometimes fringed, rays give the blossom a slight resemblance to the Japanese chrysanthemum. Long, slender, rather stiff stems fit the flower heads beautifully into floral design. Another chrysanthemum, this one from the Canary Islands, is the Paris daisy, called marguerite by the florists. It is quite shrubby, branching repeatedly, with coarsely divided leaves and flowers of yellow or white much smaller than the large blossoms of the Shasta daisy. Not only does it arrange easily, but it can be obtained the year around. Cut back the plant after flowering, and presently new growth appears. Australia has sent us the Swan River daisy, a low-growing, tender annual not related to the chrysanthemum. The small flowers, white or pink or blue, make attractive edgings or neat little tufts of color in the border. The blue daisy, a small shrub one to three feet high, bears delicate flowers much like the wild aster, or Michaelmas daisy. Formerly called agathea, it now is known botanically as felicia.

Daisies should never be glamorized in arrangements. Their gaiety and informality, their air of whimsey, suggest the old-fashioned garden.

Daisy

Daisy with Tree Branch

DAISY

Simple material in artless design can acquire distinction through well-chosen accessories. Handsome Shasta daisies, selected for their plump white cushions and bright yellow centers, are supported by small yellow daisies. Tall stalks of Spanish broom extend the design; their stems thread the arrangement with its one tone of dark color. A container of severely beautiful Chinese crackleware stands on a teakwood base; at the corner a dainty Chinese lady pays her homage to floral beauty.

DATURA

This design is built on a large scale to interpret the beauty of the datura. The flowers are set in close arrangement but not massed; the shape of each blossom is preserved. Their size can be estimated by comparing them with the long leaves of the aspidistra. Striped aspidistra mellows the contrast from light to dark. A tall, green urn of glazed pottery gives a substantial foundation of form and color.

Datura

Like most Renaissance gallants, Captain John Smith took supreme delight in perilous adventure. His own book of his exploits in the New World he wrote with that same dash which he applied to the business of living. He told, among other things, of the wildly fantastic behavior of his men after they had eaten the fruit of a strange plant. His story gave the plant the name of Jamestown weed, presently corrupted into jimson weed, the popular name which it still bears. We know today that the jimson weed, a species of datura, can induce mad antics and worse. The daturas contain strong narcotics, highly poisonous in any sizable dose and in smaller quantities producing delirious frenzies. Ancient Peruvian priests of prophetic vision are believed to have used datura seeds, which perhaps also stimulated the ravings of the Delphian oracle. A dangerous plant, indeed; yet another species is called angel's trumpet, from the white beauty of the flowers.

The daturas—some of them small plants, more of them shrubs, and a few even trees—all have large, trumpet-shaped flowers, usually white, sometimes tinged with violet, occasionally red or yellow. The leaves are very lovely: oval, shining vividly green on the upper surface, paler green below, with conspicuous vein structure depressed on the upper side of the leaf, almost channeled.

Daturas are easy to grow. The jimson weed is much too easy; it has naturalized itself throughout the United States. The angel's trumpet is tropical; in southern areas it makes a treelike shrub with large trunk and long, drooping branches covered with pendulous trumpets. It is, then, effective behind a structure that it can seem to cover.

To use in arrangements pick before the buds open, for a touch of the hand causes petal discoloration. Immerse completely before arranging the branches. The datura is suited to tall designs that give the large flowers suitable space for suspension.

Datura

Datura and Aspidistra

Delphinium

IN THE gardens of our great-grandparents the annual larkspur was a favorite. It was easy to grow, made an attractive garden display in beds or borders, and was satisfactory for cutting. This annual we still have, improved, to be sure, but unmistakably what we call old-fashioned. Dainty in flower and foliage, brightly blue or rose, it seems to belong with the bachelor's button and the garden pink. From this type of flower have been developed the showy hybrids we call delphinium. The great beauty of the delphinium has carried it to all sections of the United States, even to those areas where its success has been uncertain and difficult. It belongs in the north, where it will find seasonal cold; only in the warm southern regions is it temperamental and crotchety.

The delphinium should be planted in a deeply worked soil of excellent drainage. Whether the earth texture is heavy or light does not seem of great importance, if the preparation has been very deep in the heavy soil. The location should be sunny and open, with free circulation of air but protection from the wind. Some of the spikes grow very tall; in many varieties the stalks are too brittle to stand against the wind.

It is this height that gives the delphinium its particular value in the garden. Among the spike-producing plants it has the truest spire. In a border planting carefully graded in height and color, these spires provide a regal beauty difficult to create with other plant material. The heaviness of the spires makes the delphinium effective in vertical arrangements. Remove most or all of the foliage; it is too straggly to be attractive in the design. If other flowers are used in the composition, the delphinium probably will dominate because of its size. Choose the color combination carefully. An analogous harmony is good. For sharply dramatic effects use the blue delphinium with complementary tones.

DELPHINIUM

The delphinium is an extravagantly hybridized plant, far removed from its simple origin. Here it is given an equally sophisticated arrangement. An elaborate three-layer glass compote supports the tall placements of white delphinium and blush-pink stock. Supplementary details are fashioned with closely massed heads of green hydrangea and bunches of green grapes. An ultimate refinement is accomplished by the addition of spreading grass plumes, whose thin-spun iridescence glints in the moving air.

Delphinium

Delphinium and Daisies

Dried Arrangements

TEMPERATE

IN ALMOST any country at least one season of the year will have a scarcity of flowers. If one is mindful of the future, he can prepare for these slack periods. Most gardeners know many plant materials that in dry state retain the delicate details of form; a very few hold their natural color. These can be shaped into the same patterns used for living growth; they keep indefinitely.

The grasses afford tall, slender shapes. Among the large grasses most dramatic is the pampas with its loose plumes. The cereal grains are better lasting than the pampas, and cleaner in line. Wheat, oats, and barley have small, neat heads of seeds with long-awned beards that are their most picturesque detail. Growing wild on the sandhills of the southern part of the United States is an ornamental grass called sea oat with flat clusters of flowers that dry well. From the marshes and the ponds come lotus pods and the tall, straight cattails, valuable for the rich brown of their flower spike. Dusty fields and roadsides offer goldenrod, thistles, and dock. The dock is good for autumn arrangements because of the strength of its red-brown coloring. The prickly heads of the various thistles and thistlelike plants, especially the teasel and the artichoke, add shapes of vigorous interest to a design. Other seed containers of distinctive quality are cotton bolls with the white fluff showing at their split seams, and yucca pods. The garden contributes seed pods of the poppy and the montbretia, and a long list of flowers that dry in color. Sprays of the bells of Ireland, hydrangea heads, and the globe amaranth give neatly rounded forms; statice and the celosia retain their highly individual characteristics, the celosias even in true color. There are leaves of the magnolia and the aspidistra; nuts in plenty; acorns and oakballs; eucalyptus buds and pine cones. One can fashion designs for the entire winter.

Dried Arrangements of the Temperate Zone

DRIED ARRANGEMENT: TEMPERATE

A sheath of eucalyptus bark, its curling edges torn when sloughed by the tree, holds a spire of dried materials. All of them are common plants; all are rich with the deepened tones of fading sunlight. The tallest placement of dock, a once-despised weed of field and roadside, forms a background for the clustered umbels of yarrow in the center. Ripened heads of barley delicately link the yellow and the red-browns.

Dried Arrangements

TROPICAL

Tropical plants offer fascinating material for dried arrangements because many of the forms are unfamiliar. All of them can be obtained in the commercial market; a surprising number are produced in American greenhouses and in the gardens of the southern area of the United States.

The largest objects are palm sheaths and bamboo stalks to function either as details within impressive designs or as containers to hold the dry arrangement. The palm sheath is handsome: straw-colored on the back of the sheath and rich red-brown inside. For tall, slender features dried banana sheaths cut into narrow strips fashion into shapely furlings; the straight, lance-shaped leaf of the pandanus stands erect, as does the beautifully veined foliage of the ti. Both leaves and flowers of the dombeya shrub can be dried. The flowers, growing in closely packed heads or many-flowered clusters, can be set as if they were hydrangeas; their roundness is good above their own leaves, which are large and sharply angled, almost palmate. Another large leaf from the cecropia tree of the mulberry family places well in the foreground because of its irregular, many-lobed margin and pronounced color contrast. The white undersurface of the growing leaf dries to silver-white with dark brown above. It is very beautiful. The sea grape, or seaside plum as it is sometimes called, is a large shrub that likes sandy places, often growing along the beach. Its leaves are six or more inches wide and nearly round. Picturesque bits of the coconut palm are the familiar nuts; the rosettes, or sheaths, within which the nut was fastened; and the flowering tassels. Seed pods always are interesting. Of sufficient beauty to function as principal detail is the pod of the Ceylon morning glory, a large, rounded capsule whose richly lustrous surface has given it the not inappropriate name of wood rose. Other shapely pods come from the poinciana, the shower tree, the sterculia, and the orchid tree.

DRIED ARRANGEMENT: TROPICAL

Even dried, these materials suggest the tang of curling breakers, the opulence of southern coloring. Red-brown palm sheaths give a warm foundation. Tall ti leaves, vivid as when luxuriantly green, are encircled by twisting strips of dried banana fiber. Three dombeya leaves dip lobed edges to the table, forming a basal setting for a cluster of those most beautiful of seed pods, the Ceylon morning glory, appropriately called wood roses.

Dried Arrangements of Tropical Lands

Embryo Palm

ARRANGEMENTS of the professional designer contain marks of distinction that set them apart from attempts of the untried amateur. One expects choice flowers and leafage assembled in smart pattern so expertly that the mechanics, if there be any, do not show. Sometimes mingled with the observer's admiration is a note of perplexity: part of the material is unrecognizable; it is strange; it does not seem like vegetation. Is it some new artificial device wrought of paper or plastic? Professionals know that in any sizable plant much that is lovely is concealed from view. These interior parts—shapely in form, interesting in texture, and sometimes exquisite in color—can serve to good purpose in floral artistry. Such knowledge is taught in classes of flower arrangement; this information is part of the necessary background of the many amateur designers whose deft fingers create the beautiful displays of our flower shows.

The embryo palm is the young, unfolded leaf. In this tightly pressed blade are alternating layers of green fingers and red-brown sheath. The green is as delicate as fresh blades of grass; the sheath as fragile as the paper-thin lining of the almond shell. Fold upon fold, these convoluted layers weave an intricate pattern in form and color. At the edges the fingertips of the leaves fray out in corrugated wisps. The embryo palm is unbelievably lovely.

Use has been made in this book of other concealed plant material. The study of the agave uses the inner sheaths. One picture shows the pointed tips and the spined edges, a reasonably naturalistic view; but in the other picture the middle portions of the sheaths with square-cut tops have been folded like fat white candles, and seem as waxen. The anthurium spathes appear beside the inverted stalk of the yucca. One never should destroy a plant to obtain hidden parts; but if for any legitimate reason the plant is cut down, then its whole beauty may be utilized.

Embryo Palm

Embryo Palm with Leaves

EMBRYO PALM

This unusual design is set in an Oriental container of rich metal with curious elephant-trunk handles. Three folded leaves of the bronze heliconia form a stately background for the Colombian spathiphyllum. The showy spathes, both ivory and white or reversed to show the green undersurface, introduce the color of the main placement of embryo palm. The fantastic shapes of the palm, its twisted folds of color, the sudden caprices of its fringed margins hold endless interest.

Eucalyptus

WHEREVER the eucalyptus is grown, it is prized for its practical virtues as well as its beauty. Forests of blue gum furnish material for wooden tool parts, lumber for furniture construction and veneer finishes, and medicinal oil distilled from the leaves. Since the tree grows very rapidly, a good stand of timber can be maintained through directed cutting and sprout production from the stem. As windbreak the eucalyptus is invaluable, for the trees will thrive even when set very close. Tall and straight, gray-green or blue-green, they are beautiful in long, stately rows for street or highway planting. Unlike most trees, the eucalyptus has in its trunk an important item of beauty. The mature bark is ripe in color and texture; bark in the peeling stage—for the tree sheds its bark annually—takes fantastic shapes; the peeled trunk is creamy-white and lustrous. To drive at any time of year along a parkway planted to eucalyptus is to pursue an endless succession of beautiful forms. The flowers are fragile. They grow in small clusters—white, pink, yellow, or red—made up of petals fine as hair, like stamens; the entire blossom is delicately fleeting and the sport of the wind. The calyx cups are so highly pictorial that a cluster is as lovely as a sprig of foliage. The matured seed pods are decorative for dry material.

Unusual and dramatic arrangements can be made from the eucalyptus. If the flowers are to be used, they must be picked in the bud stage when the blossoms are about to emerge from the sheaths but still have their petals turned in like the end of a ball of yarn. They shatter almost as soon as they open. Remove much of the foliage, cut a gash in the end of the stem to help the water rise from the container, and immerse deeply.

Eucalyptus

Eucalyptus with Aucuba Leaves

EUCALYPTUS

This arrangement glitters. A brass urn, polished until it looks made of some rare, golden glass, holds one branch of flaming eucalyptus. Mature material was selected with lateral growth to suggest the three-placement pattern. Fortunately the blossoms group neatly on the main stem to provide central interest. The clusters at the ends of the side branches have been partly stripped of their stamens, leaving the shapely light-colored calyxes to catch the light. Leaves scattered loosely on the rim relieve the severity of an otherwise flat surface.

FRANCOA

This design is gentle and delicate. Though the height of the francoa is displayed, the smallness of the flowers and their fragility express daintiness. Francoa stalks turn into charming curves. No two of these several branches take precisely the same course, a circumstance that provides variety in the heavy vertical. Three gardenias complete the design, one at the base of the Dresden compote to indicate the floral garland of the ornamentation.

Francoa

Every garden needs here and there plants that are fine and delicate. They fill little pockets in the border; they furnish inconspicuous transition between units in the design. Much of the dainty growth belongs to spring, to the cool, moist air that flows through the garden at the beginning of summer when floral display is its loveliest. Any plant that in midsummer suggests the freshness of May and June is largess to the flower arranger.

The francoa is as tenuous as the blossoms of the flowering fruit trees. It is a perennial from Chile, a saxifrage. Delighting in mild temperatures, it has adapted itself to the southern areas of the United States. Farther north it is comfortable in a cool greenhouse. Wherever it can be planted permanently outdoors, it gives gentle color to the summer garden. Like most saxifrages it displays its principal foliage in a basal rosette of coarsely toothed lyre-shaped leaves. The flowers appear in close racemes at the top of slender stems two or three feet high. The four-petaled blossoms are small, usually less than an inch across, and either white or pink. The familiar species is white with the merest suggestion of pink in the center of each flower. In another variety of more robust habits the basal leaves grow on long stalks, then arch toward the ground; the flowers are pale pink, sometimes spotted or banded with white. The type used for patio planting is taller and more woody than other kinds, with crinkled leaves that contrive inconstant outlines against a brick or paved flooring; the racemes of white flowers give the plant its popular name of maiden's wreath.

Arrangements should accent the delicacy of the flower. All-white combinations of refined texture are good. Coloring either in the container or in combining material should be pastel. The stem requires shallow water in the container.

Francoa

Frangipani

IN THE remote Middle Ages, when fine gentlemen walked the knife's edge between danger and beauty, a nobleman for pretty pastime dabbled in essences. Through his elegant trifling he distilled a perfume of delicate color and entrancing odor. His name was Franchipanier. Someone, so the story goes, knowing this tale, thought his name an apt tribute to the sweet-scented plumeria of the tropics.

The frangipani, a plumeria, is a handsome shrub or low tree with long, narrow leaves, vividly green. Most of the flowers appear when the branches are bare, but when both foliage and bloom are present together the brightness of the greenery forms a beautiful background for the blossoms. The flowers are exquisite, waxy funnels whose five petals spread smoothly in a three-inch span. The typical colors are white, pale yellow, or rose, or a combination of the three, with a coral-orange species that is accounted very choice. Palest in hue at the outer edge, the petal shades delicately to the darkest tone at the center. The short stem holding each flower is a vivid rose, and that tone extends as a stripe on the back of the petal. Before the flower opens, the bud stands erect on its short stem, tightly furled to a sharp point at the tip. As it matures, the petals spread ever so slowly, revealing in alternating slits of color the tones of the upper and the under sides. The life of each flower is brief, with an almost constant fall of blossoms to the ground. The Tahitians plant the frangipani among their graves to provide a blanket of soft color and waxen purity. For this reason the Polynesians call the plumeria the graveyard flower and will not wear it.

The stalks, even the small stems, exude a heavy, creamy juice that drops freely from any cut surface. To replace this milk, the plant material must be given immediate and complete immersion to prevent wilting.

FRANGIPANI

A banana stalk has been hollowed to resemble the Japanese bamboo container. Here it is preferable to the bamboo, since its pink tint is the pink of the frangipani. A modification of Japanese design shows the flowering branches with the blossoms in natural growth against their own leaves. Also according to nature several blossoms have dropped from their stems to rest upon the table. No tree is more Polynesian than this frangipani; no pattern more Oriental than this style, though the Orientals would not use this abundance of floral material.

Frangipani

Frangipani with Hibiscus

Fruit

HE PROBLEMS confronting the artist who works with fruit are those of basic design, as indicated in the page of vegetable arrangements. The question of immediate concern with fruit is the practical one of durability. How long is the arrangement intended to last? Is it to be used for a single occasion? Or will it remain a few days? Most vegetables have fairly good keeping qualities. The hard fruits retain their firmness, but soft fruits will not linger. One decaying peach can ruin a composition; and any attempt to replace spoiled fruit with fresh is all too likely to destroy the entire design.

One of the delights of working with fruit is the endless variety within a kind. The citrus fruits, for example, have the giant grapefruit and the tiny kumquat; the yellow lemon and the green lime; the large ball of the navel orange and the small, flattened tangerine; then the citron, unlike all the others. Another point of interest is the differing effects secured by a slight manipulation of the fruit. The soft color of plums and prunes when first they are picked from the tree, as if veiled in gray mist, is caused by a fine, powdery coating on the skin. Rub the skin, or wash it, and the color emerges true and vivid. Always try the damask effect first; for once the powder is removed the grayness cannot be restored. Many grapes also have a bloom. Fine details of fruit structure often add interest. An apple when featured in an arrangement is more important if turned to show the stem; a short sprig with a leaf or two attached combines well with the fruit. Leaf material may be used with fruit, whether it be the natural foliage or a harmonious selection, because leafage is a normal part of fruit growth. A study of old fruit prints will suggest pleasing accessories.

Fruit

FRUIT

For festive occasions a dressed-up design of fruit will contain some floral material. This arrangement, intended for a gift, is placed suitably in a basket. It has been planned chiefly for color harmony. The only fruit used is grapes placed against a dramatic inverted triangle of ti leaves, some of them furled at their tips into tight little rolls. Gardenias and their leaves provide a final decorative accent.

Geranium

Our colorful garden geranium has been a long time on the way. From its beginning in South Africa, where it was cultivated by the English settlers and the Dutch, it moved to England late in the seventeenth century. Europeans were delighted with the small bright flowers. Their hybridizers produced variant forms of sufficient interest to stimulate a wide interest in the plant; in fact, the growing of geraniums became a popular fad, and several species of the show types resulted. We know today that these flowers are not geraniums botanically, but pelargoniums; the two plants are quite disparate. Since custom sanctions usage, the name geranium has been used so long that geraniums they are everywhere except in solid books of learning.

Today in the United States the fancy-type geraniums are admired widely, but geraniums in general are not appreciated as they should be. The common or bedding geranium, the zonal, is loved the world over. It is a folk flower, patiently nursed through cold winters as a kitchen pot-plant or a window specimen in regions of rigorous weather. In temperate climates, where it grows in the garden, it makes a large, bushy shrub. The ivy-leaved geranium is a much weaker plant of straggling habits, but very attractive, with its bright leaves lobed in sharp angles and its delicately tinted flowers of white, pink, rose, and lavender. It is used in hanging baskets, for curbside plantings, or for cover growth wherever trailing or pendent stems are desired. The scented-leaf geraniums are grown for their foliage. The leaves are usually interesting in shape and often soft and velvety in texture. The sweet geraniums go by names suggested by their fragrance—lemon, rose, nutmeg.

For arrangements largely defoliate the branches. The short-stemmed, bunchy growth of the leaves confuses the lines of the design.

Geranium

Geranium with Scabiosas

GERANIUM

The angular pattern is not used frequently in floral design. In this arrangement a modification has been developed. The chief placement is formed of a rich stalk of rose pentstemon slightly curved at the tip to break the rigidity of the line. The base is more deeply curved to reach the table. Brilliant red geraniums, the common garden variety, are clustered at the angle of the flowers, where their glowing color will attract immediate attention.

GERBERA

Subtle color gradations distinguish this arrangement. A vertical line of apricot-colored quill chrysanthemums stands between two rows of orange-red gerberas, paralleling one of the rows and contiguous to it. The two placements of gerberas meet at the base but diverge sharply to afford room for the short stalks of francoa which also fill in the base to an attractive line and soften the rigid perpendicular.

Gerbera

CHOICE among ray flowers is the gerbera. Native of Asia and South Africa, of tropical and warm temperate regions, it has been established slowly in the United States. Any flat ray flower carelessly is named daisy, frequently with a qualifying word to distinguish it from other pseudo-daisies. Thus the gerbera often is called African daisy, a meaningless term because many ray flowers live in Africa. If a popular name must be used, the gerbera should be called Transvaal daisy or Barberton daisy.

The gerbera is a tender perennial grown outdoors in warm belts but in colder areas restricted to interior planting, either in the greenhouse or potted for window decoration. As a house plant it is usually a winter bloomer, producing a long succession of bright flowers. The plant is neat. The leaves, eight to ten inches long and deeply cut, make a clustered base for the tall flowering stems. The blossoms are three inches across, both single and double forms. In the doubles the petals of the second, or inner, row are very short; they build a low, flat cushion in the center of the corolla. The flowers range in color from white and cream through pale yellow and salmon, coral, and terra cotta to deep red—warm crowns above the gray-green foliage at their base. The plants bear heavily enough to provide cut flowers for the house while maintaining a good display in the garden.

The flowers wilt after cutting. To condition them for arrangements immerse the stems deeply, but for only a short time, watching to see when the flower heads stiffen. If left too long in deep water, the stem starts to rot. The gerbera looks best in informal arrangements, either alone or with selected foliage. Combining flowers must be selected carefully for harmonizing color.

Gerbera

Gerbera with Aucuba Leaves

Ginger: Red

Someone in the remote Oriental past, digging for aromatic roots dear to the Eastern palate, observed the shape of the object in his hand and gave it a name. When the commercial value of this root eventually was discovered, the identification of the plant appeared in the usual classical form as the Greek word *zingiberis*, which is the source, by easy shifts, of our word *ginger*. Some dictionaries trace the word no further than the Greek; but etymologists find the Greek word probably a translation of an ancient vernacular Indian word meaning *horn-shaped*. The root of the ginger is a rhizome something like the rhizome of the iris and indeed horn-shaped. The plant is so old that no one is altogether sure of its origin: perhaps India, perhaps China, but certainly somewhere in the dank tropical forests of southeastern Asia. Western civilization valued the root even as did the Oriental. The dried rhizome furnishes substances for medicinal preparations; the green rhizome is the source of our spice; and the tenderest, most juicy rhizomes are preserved in pickling syrup to become candied ginger. The root, then, is a means of wealth, just as the leaves and flowers are known for their decorative beauty.

In the United States the ginger grows freely through the southern areas. Farther north it is a warm greenhouse plant, attractive at all stages of growth. The young shoots, before they leaf out, resemble delicate reeds and, like reeds, can be used in floral design. In maturity the stems develop into strong stalks with handsome foliage. The flower growth is sheathed, usually spikelike or conelike, with one flower emerging from each bract.

The red ginger likes a shady, moist location. A tall grower of rich appearance from base to tip of highest stem, it provides great splashes of color for the tropical garden, with its spikes of bright crimson which flower for most of the year.

GINGER: RED

A sweeping rhythm permeates the recurrent unit of this design. Four leaves of the ti plant, close set to overlap, rise in regularly increasing heights, only to be overtopped by stalks of red ginger similarly placed and likewise increasing in height. The red ginger covering the base of the ti leaves repeats the pattern of arrangement, which in final appearance shapes the foundation through the overlapping of the rolled ti leaves.

Ginger: Red

Ginger with Croton Leaves

Ginger: Shell

THE GINGER of the United States is one of the most fragrant flowers in the garden. The loosely clustered blossoms are two-toned, light yellow, and cream. Though they grow easily and need no unusual care, they nevertheless convey a feeling of exotic elegance.

Other very interesting types of ginger are readily available on the commercial market. The torch ginger is altogether magnificent. Its leaf stalks are tall, ten feet or more, bearing leaves of bronze-green. Well below the level of the leaf stalks are the flower stems, with large cones of red or pink blossoms, quite waxen in textural effect. When one comes suddenly upon a group of these plants in a shaded portion of the garden, their flower bracts vivid against their own foliage, one readily can appreciate the popular name, torch ginger.

Another variety characteristic of tropical gardens is the Kahili ginger. The plant itself is somewhat unkempt in appearance, unlike the close, neat foliage of most gingers. The flower stalks are taller than the leafage, with quite remarkable blossoms of yellow flowers from which extend long, bright red filaments, the whole effect reminiscent of the feathered rods used by early chieftains in their ceremonies.

Among the delicate species is the shell ginger. The stalks, tall sometimes to twelve feet, with smooth, slender leaves like a large wild grass, arch to the ground in the most graceful manner. The blooms grow in slim cones, the bracts a waxen white, with flowers opened ever so slightly to show the red and yellow coloring inside the pink of the outer surface.

Any arrangement of ginger should depict the tropics. Use ginger alone with foliage. Completely defoliate the stalks to prolong the life of the arrangement and to simplify the design, because the leaves grow horizontally from the stalk in a bunched thatch. After conditioning they may be used as separate units of the design. The torch ginger is easiest to arrange, since the flower stalk is leafless.

Ginger: Shell

Ginger with Croton Leaves

GINGER: SHELL

Restrained line and delicate color characterize this arrangement. The principal placement includes two opened racemes and a stalk whose two buds have parted slightly at the tip to show a point of color, the flower within the sheath. This line is supported by strips of banana sheath, extremely glossy, rolled into tight curls. Flat strips slashed obliquely connect the vertical details and the two sprays of the ginger that depend from the rim of the container.

Gladiolus

OVER the sun-drenched plains of early Greece the air flowed tirelessly in endless ripples. Little gay curls of color ran lightly before the wind through the fields of crested grain. The corn lilies had blossomed. Centuries later men of valor looked upon the fields. Familiar with the tools that forge death rather than life, they recognized the shape of the long, green blades behind the gay blossoms: the same flowers, but to them—sword lilies; and to us also, sword lilies—the gladiolus.

Available the year around in market, the gladiolus is also easily grown at home. Planted in the cutting garden in straight rows, spaced a few weeks apart, it should be treated like a vegetable. If the soil is good—preferably a sandy loam—if the irrigation is regular and cultivation frequent, the plants will produce a long sequence of color. For ornamentation the gladiolus gives splendid accent to the border. Succession can be secured here by careful choice of early and late varieties. Horticulturists recommend the lifting of corms after the foliage has died at the end of the blooming season to ensure dormancy. A heavy bloomer like the gladiolus needs rest.

The blossoms appear on tall stalks, the spike of somewhat funnel-shaped flowers held closely between two leafy bracts. Among the thousands of named forms is almost infinite variation. The huge exhibition type and the tiny miniatures less than an inch across are equally resultant from careful development. The flowers have also been bred to shape, with ruffled or fringed or twisted petals. Solid colors vie with blossoms in flecked or veined markings.

Pick the gladiolus when only the lowest bud is opening. Day by day the flowers unfurl toward the tip, looking their best in vertical patterns. Since the gladiolus can be combined with any kind of flower and will keep for days, it is highly prized by garden lovers.

Gladiolus

Gladiolus and Water Lilies

[1 6 3]

GLADIOLUS

The container is an essential part of this design. A cylinder of clear glass is partly filled with umbels of blue agapanthus, which give a solid base of color. At the top of the container a Y-shaped holder secures the tall stalks of delphinium and gladiolus, which are mingled deftly to obtain a pleasing color blend. The Y-holder is concealed by the dependent sprays of gladiolus and agapanthus blossoms.

Heliconia

EVERY foot of Greece is storied ground. Mountains particularly fired the imagination of the early Greek, and of mountains there was an abundance: for protection from neighbors, almost invariably enemies; for retreat; as abiding place for their deities. One of them, Mount Helicon, was the home of the Muses, those fastidious maidens who presided over the arts. It takes a very superior type of elegance to live up to the name Helicon, but the heliconia is quite untroubled by its designation.

It is a member of the large banana family, more entirely tropical than the true banana. In the United States it is wholly a greenhouse resident; but in its home environment it grows tall, though never to such height as the banana. The leaves emerge directly from the ground; they are large and handsome, and the several types exhibit an interesting difference in color. The most common variety is vividly green with prominent vein-ribbing. A closely related form is striped, sometimes with gold beside the veins, even the stem being striped gold and green, sometimes with pink. One of the largest types has leaves of pale green mottled with gray. In all these forms the foliage is part of the plant.

The floral growth appears on long stalks below the leaves. The true flowers are very colorful; yet the bracts, or flower sheaths, are even more brilliant than the flowers themselves. The blossoms most commonly seen in the commercial market are red or orange with very large sheaths of scarlet and black. Other species have bracts of pale pink edged with yellow, then green; or rich red bordered with green. The flower, together with its sheath, looks remarkably like a bird; hence the plant is sometimes called the false bird of paradise. Arrange it very simply, either alone or with nothing but other foliage material of tropical characteristics. It keeps for weeks.

Heliconia

Heliconia and Aspidistra Leaves

HELICONIA

This vertical arrangement of heliconia expresses the remotely exotic. Three stalks show vividly against a column made by obliquely slashing symmetrical lengths of peeled layers of the banana stalk. The base of the design is filled with loops of the same glossy banana stripping. Dark-green blades set among the heliconia to relieve the sameness of the yellow-green are aspidistra leaves. The container is a primitively carved temple bowl from Polynesia.

Hibiscus

In the golden age of Rome, while Augustus was establishing the empire, the poet Vergil named a flower. He called it hibiscus, though he did not use the word precisely in our sense. To him, hibiscus meant mallow; to us, it designates only one genus of the mallow family. That it was used at all is the first important thing: one more link between our civilization and the mighty past. Second in interest is the fact that the name of a beautiful flower was chosen by a man who understood beauty, who worked in an era devoted among other things to the cultivation of art. Like Vergil, we admire the flower that we call hibiscus.

The shrub is large. Normally the strong, woody branches emerge from the main stalk close to the ground, but by careful cutting the shrub can be pruned into a conventional tree. The flowers are large and bell-shaped, each one carried singly on a short stem. In the center of each blossom is its most conspicuous feature, a long, red column bearing the pollen. The color range is extensive, from pure white through the various tints and the deep tones of every hue except blue and purple. The flowers occur in both single and double forms, some with petals almost like crinkled paper.

Never many at a time, the blossoms open during a great part of the year. Each flower lasts from early morning until sunset. If the flower is needed for evening use, pick early before it has unfurled and store it in a cool, dark place all day. It will then open under the evening lights. The hibiscus keeps equally well with or without water. It is, accordingly, one of the few flowers that profit by artificial devices of arrangement. Strung on slim reeds, the blooms can be fashioned into stylized designs. Dramatic effects can be secured through the use of geometric compositional patterns.

Hibiscus

Hibiscus with Leaves

HIBISCUS

Since hibiscus flowers last dry as well as in water, the arranger may indulge his fancy for artificial manipulation. Flowers of apricot hibiscus strung on coco sticks are set in the container as if they were conventional flower stalks. For foundation material croton leaves were chosen, since their beautiful yellow vein system supplements the tone of the hibiscus. One flower is set inside the container of clear Swedish glass to continue the color to the base.

HOLLY

This arrangement of holly expresses simply yet very beautifully the joy of the Christmas season. To suggest tree growth, branches of the bright foliage are set in loose informality in a large jar of green Italian glass. One small cluster of berries is the only interruption to the glossiness of the foliage. But the small artificial tree built of closely massed carnations in the precise color of holly berries is a novel detail in holiday decoration.

Holly

Books, old prints, and carols all hang the holly high at Christmas time. Garden and forest have no brighter gift to the short, darkened daylight of winter than its shining leaves and berries. Traditional on Christmas cards and most beautiful of the many varieties is the English holly, which in its homeland becomes a tall tree. In the United States, where it is not so hardy as the native species, it succeeds best in the northwest. It is a pyramidal tree of neatly compact growth. The short-stemmed leaves are lustrous on the upper surface, with wavy margin edged with strong prickles. Equally brilliant are the berries; larger than the fruit of American varieties, they are borne in dense clusters. Some hybrids have variegated leaves, one with narrow silver margin, another whose blades are mottled with gray spots and finished with a narrow outer band of yellow.

The Japanese holly is a handsome shrub more branched than either the English or the native American kinds. Fine-toothed leaves on some types are elliptical; on others, enough broader at base to be almost wedge-shaped. The berries are black like those of the American plant called ink-berry. But though both these shrubs are beautiful, with unusually attractive foliage, we prefer the red fruit for holiday decoration. The American holly most nearly like the beautiful English tree is tall, not so spreading as its cousin, and sharply pyramidal at the top. The leaves are not so shining nor the berries so red as those of the English variety, but it is quite vivid enough to make a brave show.

Holly is difficult to keep. Either float in water or wrap in wet paper until it is to be used. The sheen of the leaf is so brilliant that it adds sparkle to any other foliage with which it is combined.

Holly

Hollyhock

A WORLD of burnished glitter seeks occasional escape from too much chrome. It would turn from the shapely precision of the formal garden to the quaintness of our grandmother's front yard. Behind our zestful esteem for our own machined civilization waits the stanch tranquillity of settled achievement, of the long established. Hollyhocks grew in England when Sir Francis Drake roamed the seas. In that same sixteenth century they were ancient in China, cultivated probably for more than ten centuries before Europe saw them. They seem to belong to a world of slow, informal living.

Leaning against a fence or a garden wall, backed by a trellis or a house —the house preferably white, a cottage or pillared colonial—they suit their scene. They should be grouped. A single plant, despite its grace, is much too slender to fit attractively into any garden pattern. Nor, when grouped, should they stand in the perennial border. Their surprising loveliness is overly conspicuous for a neighborhood where beauty is progressively effected without rivalry. Use them to fill an empty space or to screen an unsightly area. The very tall varieties like something to lean against.

The hollyhock plant needs a rich soil, well drained, not too light, with full sun even to its base. When the lower leaves are in shade, the plant does not prosper. That foliage clothing the stem from the ground to the flower buds is part of the stately beauty of the hollyhock. The leaves are large enough to create an illusion of substance and strength appropriate to the height. The flowers appear at the top of the hairy stalk, like all raceme effects opening successively toward the tip. The color range is wide: lovely pastels in cream, true pink, salmon; deep tones of scarlet, red, and maroon.

Strip the stalk of its leaves, then immerse the entire branch in water until conditioned. The freshened blossoms will glamorize the arrangement as surely as do the camellias.

HOLLYHOCK

This arrangement is a monochromatic harmony in formal balance. Long sprays of rose larkspur create the main outlines of the pattern, with the lateral branches more loosely spaced than is expected in formal design. The principal feature is the massing of pink hollyhocks in the center with their extension into the vertical placement and irregularly into the two lateral placements. Small branches of pink stock supplement the hollyhocks as transitions to the darker larkspur.

Hollyhock with Leaves

Hydrangea

WHOEVER named the hydrangea had a faculty of nice discernment. Better, probably, than most of us he saw the fruit of the shrub. Our tidy fingers clip the hydrangea heads as soon as the flowers wither, for the drying petals are very unsightly. Then many of the flowers, especially those of our beautiful modern hybrids, are sterile and will not set fruit. But long ago, when plants were simple and unmodified, even the hydrangea followed the natural pattern from bud to seed; the tiny flower produced its correspondingly small fruit, a lobed capsule that, when ripe, split open at the top, forming a cup-shaped pod and giving the namer his word—water vessel.

Our forefathers admired the shrub we call the common hydrangea; its large masses of bloom edged the north porch or filled the wall space under an east window. Today, even while using this plant because it is handsome, inexpensive, and easy to grow, we covet any number of the wonderful new varieties. The color range has been extended. Some hybrids that flower as creamy white or blue or rose turn green in late summer. The pink and the rose hues are more vivid than formerly, some with single flowers an inch across. Blue tones, once obtained by liberal feedings of iron, now are constant and true in great, rounded masses of soft blue or rosy violet. Among the flat clusters is an exquisite specimen, the center a densely crowded growth of tiny blue or blue-violet flowers, the margin a single row of white flowers, large and conspicuous. Any of these types set in rich, moist soil in partial shade will make good-sized shrubs.

The hydrangea has been little used for flower arrangements, because it wilts. Complete immersion conditions it for long use in a design. Because of its size and coloring it needs no supporting material. It looks best alone with its own foliage or with other very simple leafage.

Hydrangea

Hydrangea with Crotalaria

HYDRANGEA

Often the simplest things are the loveliest. Clusters of colorful hydrangea flowers, both common and brilliant hybrid varieties, no two of the same tone value, are placed to secure attractive color juxtaposition. Several hydrangea leaves show their dark-green tips as separators between the heads of blossoms. The container is concealed within the hollow roll of bark, whose nubbly surface offers a rugged contrast to the sleekness of the hydrangeas.

Iris

Juno, the queen of the Olympians, had as her personal messenger the loveliest of the younger deities. On fragile wings as delicately tinted as the cloud stuff of early morning, the maiden goddess flitted on swift duty. Her filmy garments were splashed with the seven colors of the sky. Lightly she ran down the rainbow bridge from Olympus. Iris brought the colors of heaven to the dim earth to be captured by a flower. The prismatic quality of the iris flowers gives them a distinctive beauty. It is not merely the endless variations, the innumerable color combinations that make them engagingly lovely; it is, in part, the shimmer of the petals against the moving air. No other plant approaches the color richness of the iris.

Though the iris is a very old plant of wide distribution, all development of importance belongs to this century. One thing we have learned is proper planting. The bearded iris needs a well-drained situation in full sun. It will grow in any good soil; for very fine flowers the earth should be dressed occasionally with bonemeal, never with manure. Only during the blooming season does it require much water; the rhizomes should be irrigated sparingly during the rest period. The beardless iris is quite different in its demands. It likes a heavier soil and much water at all times. Some of the beardless varieties are swamp plants; as such, they make lovely planting for pools.

The iris with its own foliage is quite sufficient for beautiful arrangements. If other material is used, it should be small in size or restrained in color. The slender watsonia is effective. Pick the iris in bud stage with no more than one open blossom. As others open, remove the withered ones to show the attractive angular stem.

IRIS

This arrangement shows a severely mannered design. In the taller portion
long stalks of watsonias stand before iris leaves precisely spaced in ascending verticals to the pointed tip of the spire. Two-toned irises fill the central
portion of the column. The other section of the arrangement uses only
the iris and the footing of watsonias. In this portion the iris leaves reverse
the position of the blades of the first placement.

Iris

Iris and Equisetum

Ivy

ALL of us have some association for ivy. Perhaps it is green leaves fingering their way along the red bricks of our university halls; or a tall, slim tree made still taller, yet more slender by the cloak of pointed green close-wrapped about the branches; or only the mantled tower of poetry and romance. Although we think, always, of English ivy, in sober fact the plant belongs not merely to England, not even to all of Europe alone, but to north Africa, to Asia as well, from the western portion through central Asia to Japan.

The ivy is a highly ornamental evergreen vine that climbs by means of aerial roots. It makes its way over brick and masonry by clinging to their irregularities; but it does not succeed too well on smooth wood. It is useful for screening unsightly fences or hiding open trellises. On the ground its runners weave pleasant covers for woodland areas. Small bits of ivy rooted in water are attractive in hanging baskets suspended in the porch or a shaded window. For the ivy dislikes sun. It will grow in almost any earth, though preferring a rich soil with abundant moisture. Ivy, one discovers, is not always plain dark green. In the most ordinary species the under surface of the leaf is a paler green than the upper, sometimes a yellowish green. Quite a showy type has small, rather dull green leaves margined with creamy white and striped with red or pink. Another striking color combination has white veining in a dark green background. We do not lack for diversity in the ivy.

For smooth surfaces that ivy cannot climb we have the Virginia creeper, sometimes called American ivy, and the Boston or Japanese ivy, vines that cling by means of tiny adhesive tendrils.

Ivy makes beautiful naturalistic designs. Pendent arrangements in silhouette against a plain wall space create cool beauty that will last for days if the ivy has been given deep immersion.

Ivy

IVY

Ivy looks best in designs that suggest its growth. It combines easily with material that climbs or hangs pendent. This ivy patterned with the trumpet vine shows the pliant grace of both vines. Through vivid color the massing of blossoms at the top of the old lamp directs attention to the important features of the ivy arrangement: the looped branch and the sprig that rests on the table.

Jacaranda

More people are familiar with the jacaranda than with many of the flowering trees. Perhaps because it quickly reaches tree size, it is a general favorite for home gardens as well as public parks. Indigenous to South America, it has lived in the United States so long that we forget its Brazilian origin. With no particular tastes in soil it will grow in almost any sunny location that permits lusty arm-stretching apart from overfriendly neighbors. The tall, slightly spreading tree affords very agreeable shade in the summer months. Not completely deciduous, bare of foliage only in early spring, it is good for street planting. The leaves are lacelike, finely cut and elegant enough to invite admiration even when there are no flowers. The blossoms, however, are the chief reason for the popularity of the jacaranda. They grow in large panicles at the ends of the branches, fifty or more to a cluster, loosely set so that each small bloom is seen as an individual. Since the flowering is profuse at the height of the season, the whole wide canopy of the top is festooned with plumes of color hung against the lacework of the leaves. The effect is excitingly lovely. Yet each blossom by itself is delicate, almost fragile. One knows it cannot hold its place upon the branch. The colors are refined, a tranquil blue or violet. When the single flowers loose their transient hold upon the stem to spiral lightly to the earth one by one, or when they are swung out by the wind, they fabricate a finely textured ground cover far beyond the spread of the tree. Then the garden is as softly blue underfoot as the sky is blue above.

Pick the jacaranda in bud, then completely immerse; otherwise the flowers will drop from the arrangement.

Jacaranda

Jacaranda and Lilies

JACARANDA

This floral material has been closely massed to intensify the color of the jacaranda. The lovely clusters form the main placements of this floral column at top and bottom. In both positions contrasting white lilies border the beautiful purple. Between these two groups and surrounded by its leaves is a rosy head of hybrid hydrangea that tones with the jacaranda. The vase, pale as the lilies and slender as the floral column, prolongs the pillar effect.

JACOBINIA

This arrangement shows how simple combining flowers fill a space that might be disturbing if unoccupied and yet in no way compete with the main interest of the design. The unusual growth of the jacobinia is clearly displayed, permitting the sprays of abelia to combine harmoniously with the line pattern. Warm brown in the alabaster vase and the abelia calyxes, from which many of the flowers have dropped, sharpens the red of the jacobinia.

Jacobinia

THE JACOBINIA is distributed widely through the tropical regions of the American continents from Mexico south through Bolivia and Brazil. In the southern United States it grows easily outdoors. As a greenhouse plant or potted, it can be kept suitably small for room decoration, but at home in the tropics it is a shrub five or six feet tall and oddly interesting in appearance. The smooth, slender stalks, very leggy if unrestrained, can be pruned sufficiently when the flowers are cut to keep the plant shapely. The leaves grow in pairs, set oppositely on the stem. They are oval, five or six inches long, and very handsome. The upper surface is a lively green marked with an elaborate network of veins so deeply depressed that the leaf fabric looks slightly puckered between them. On the lighter green of the undersurface the veins show boldly a deep rose color. The leaves stand out slightly from the main stem, then arch sharply downward, exaggerating the slenderness of the shrub.

The flowers are held in small conelike bracts, the same vivid green of the leaves. One blossom behind each scale of the cone shows at first a mere point of color, then grows rapidly into a long two-petaled blossom until the cone is a small fountain of riotous color. The flowers are very showy; crimson, rose, rose-purple, scarlet, and orange-yellow are the prevailing tones.

The plant is not difficult to grow. Because it is straggly and rather brittle, it needs protection from the wind. Set it in good soil, give it plenty of water during the growing and flowering season, treating it much like a fuchsia or a begonia, and it will produce a long succession of blossoms. For arrangements cut the branches when the flower first shows tips of color in the cone, then immerse the entire branch in water. It is sufficiently interesting in itself to shape into dramatic designs.

Jacobinia

Jacobinia and Chrysanthemums

Kniphofia

For bold landscape effects nothing is much more startling than the kniphofia. In its native wilderness before the days of traveled roads it must have seemed a torch to light the traveler. Native of Africa, it grows widely through the southern section and on the highlands of the tropical regions. Many of the most interesting forms are known only in their wild state and never have been seen outside their native settlements. In cultivation they cross so readily through natural pollenization that it is difficult to sort out the variant forms. Identification of the plant by name is confusing. Originally called tritoma, it now is known botanically as kniphofia. Since the commercial world has been slow in accepting the change, usually it is labeled and sold as tritoma. The popular names vary with location but are sufficiently descriptive, so that the flower easily is recognized, whether it be called red-hot poker, flame thrower, or torch lily.

It is this fiery brilliance of the plant that gives it position in the garden. Only where a tall, very showy mass is desired will the kniphofia be grown. The foliage is rather unattractive, with long, narrow leaves that start upright but midlength abandon the effort to stand and lop to the ground in awkward confusion. The flower stalks display no such indecision; from the disorder at their feet they rise four and five feet, topped by a flowering head of small tubular blossoms, one hundred or so, that point sharply down, closely overlapping in shingle effect, and all most brilliant in color, vivid tones of orange, yellow, red, and lime green.

Condition the material for arrangement by immersing the stems but not the blossoms. To obtain cunning curves in the stems, immerse the stalks horizontally, turning the flower to the light. Moving the light source induces the stem to bend at any desired point.

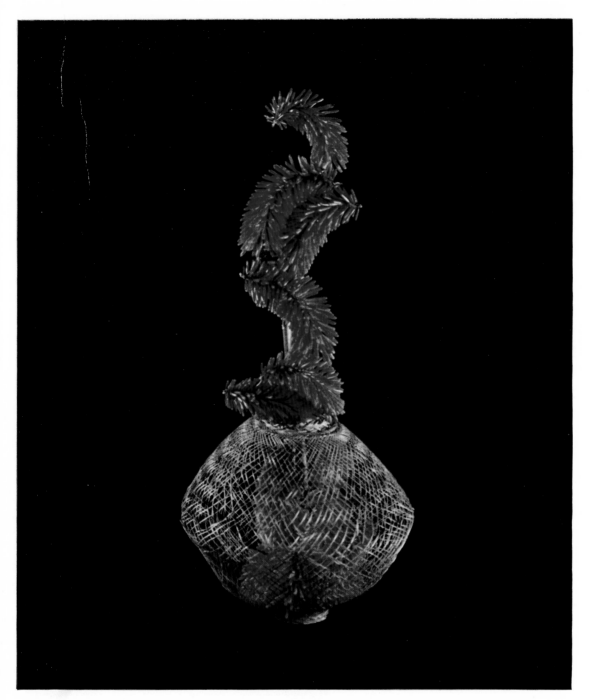

KNIPHOFIA

A floral artist does not choose startling plant material without reason. He may want a florid effect; he may wish even to surprise. The most exciting results he will secure by relying chiefly on his spectacular material and working it into effortless line patterns. Yet, placed against a plain, dark background, the kniphofia is gorgeous. In this design the spiral within the split-bamboo container becomes a flaming emergence.

Kniphofia

Kniphofia and Castor Bean

Larkspur

THE LARKSPUR is a member of the delphinium family. We try to distinguish between the tall, gorgeous perennials and the small but beautiful old-fashioned annuals by a difference in name. The hybridized beauties we call delphinium; the small plants, larkspur. The annual is slender and rather loose in growth. Easily raised from seed and granted a long flowering period, it can be planted to give either early summer or autumn bloom. Several of the most attractive varieties are natives of the western United States.

Blue is the characteristic larkspur color, ranging from the lightest of tints to deep purple. Other kinds are pale or deep rose, scarlet, and bright red. The white larkspur is especially attractive, its blossoms seeming all the whiter above the fine-cut leaves. Delphinium foliage is bold in pattern, but that of the larkspur is dainty. It often appears in stocky bunches at the joints of the stems; but though the mass may be intrusively evident the leaf itself is refined, almost like a thin line.

The larkspur is good material for the border. It blends well because its colors are not extreme; they are as nearly pure as can be found in flowers. In floral arrangements one expects to see the larkspur used alone or in combination with other common garden flowers; however, its unobtrusive verticality and clean color enable it to unite suitably with any blossom of congenial color. The pink shades, or blue, shape into smooth monochromatic designs. The rose tints are beautiful with white flowers; blue larkspur and salmon-colored phlox are lovely together. The slender spikes above a low massing of round flower-faces like scabiosas or garden pinks or marguerites can resemble the gay flower prints in old art books. Choose a simple container and an informal design. If the foliage is bunchy, it should be removed.

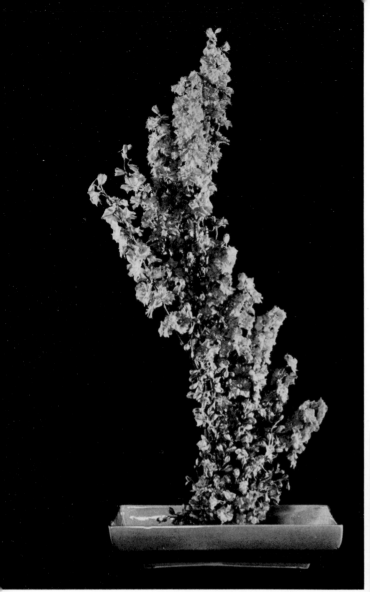

Larkspur

Larkspur and Carnations

LARKSPUR

A smartly contemporary effect is conveyed in this arrangement of larkspur, by combination with the handsome caladium leaves and the use of a container of modern design. The line on the striping of the container is prolonged into the line of the larkspur through the spiraling of the color. The vigor of the design results further from an extreme emphasis upon the verticals, secured through the slenderness of the container and the brilliant midvein of the leaves.

Lilac

A STUDY of remote kinship reveals interesting, sometimes incongruous relationships. The olive we welcome with relish; but if a completely inedible shrub like the lilac, loved for its delicately scented flowers, can belong to that same olive family, then an occasional excursion into the domain of floral heredity might disclose the whimsical or the bizarre.

The common lilac is a far traveler, originating in Asia, probably near the Caucasus or Afghanistan, and appearing early in eastern Europe. By the sixteenth century it was established in England. Quite naturally, then, it appeared in America in colonial gardens. Today it is distributed through the eastern United States. In the West, where it is not comfortable, it is infrequently grown in nostalgic memory of a dearly loved home. The West has its lilac, a small, very refined wild shrub that cloaks the mountain sides with white or smoky blue.

In regions of its choice the lilac is easily grown. It prefers a fertile, well-drained soil with sun. Feedings of bonemeal and manure will stimulate heavy flower-production, especially if the shrub is pruned every three years. The lilac makes a shrub so large that an average garden accommodates but one or two specimens. In extended landscapes it is beautiful in groups for massed color and fragrance. The color range is very short; white, red, lilac, or purple are the usual tones. The bright-green foliage is handsome enough to be attractive in arrangements. Complete branches, only sufficiently defoliated to show the large panicles of flowers to good advantage, make showy designs for a single occasion. If the arrangement is to be kept for several days, completely defoliate the branch and immerse in water to condition the blossoms. Many of the spring flowers combine well with the lilac, particularly if a color harmony is desired. Hyacinths or scilla, for their similarity of form, or tulips and stock: all can easily be secured wherever lilacs are found.

Lilac.   Lilac and Tulips

LILAC

Common garden material combined with lilac is worked into an arrangement intended to be viewed from all sides. Stock, Dutch iris, and hydrangeas have been arranged in a close tone-pattern. Orchid stock between the
deep shades of the lilac and the central placement forms a transition to the
blue hydrangeas of one lateral and the pink hydrangeas of the other. Blue
has been maintained in the iris by removing the yellow-spotted falls to
avoid a spattering of yellow points.

LILY: PLAIN

These flowers rise in a sweeping curve that suggests the circle. Easter lilies
establish the main placement, the only line to complete the arc. Constant
variation in the position of the trumpets faces no two in the same direction; and the line ends, as it began, with the point of a not-yet-opened
bud. The glow of the orange lilies is enriched by the near-complementary
blue-violet made with hydrangeas. Sharply contrasted colors were introduced to intensify the purity of the white lilies.

Lily: Plain

ARTISTS whose perception outranges the eye, whose insight plumbs the eternal verities, have used the lily as a symbol of ultimate beauty and goodness. From the paintings of the Italian Renaissance to Rossetti's damozel leaning over the parapet of heaven, the flower has meant exquisite perfection. Perhaps it is our quailing before the supreme that makes us hesitant to grow lilies in our gardens. They are often difficult to manage; for they exhibit sharp prejudices and bicker among themselves over locations. The gardener must consult the preferences of each variety, then provide the environment and the care to suit each individual taste. All of them need a light loam with good drainage; many prefer a ground cover at their feet; but some like sun in their faces, while others enjoy filtering shadows.

Best known is the Easter lily. Growing in the garden above a green underfooting or massed in tall containers within the church, through the waxen purity of its trumpets it discloses the sheer radiance inherent in austere glory. The Madonna lily is as severely white as the Easter lily. The trumpets cluster at the top of three-foot stalks, with many more blossoms to the stalk than are found in the Easter lily, each held by a very short stem. This flower belongs to Asia and southern Europe; it is the blossom generally seen in European paintings. Another stately lily is the regal, of Chinese derivation. It grows to five feet, with large clusters of long trumpets white inside, shading delicately to a yellow throat, but lilac or purple on the outer side of the perianth. The exquisite blending of tones in the blossoms above the mellow green of the foliage gives the regal a ripe richness of beauty. Fortunately for the gardener this lily is hardy and adapts itself easily to permanent planting.

Lily: Plain

Lily and Cane Grass

Lily: Variegated

DAPPLED lilies have an exotic quality. Splashes of brilliant color on the waxen surface call to mind exquisite French medallions painted on ivory. Through extensive hybridization we enjoy almost unlimited choice in both form and hue.

One of the best known of the mottled beauties is the auratum, the golden-banded lily of Japan. The long white trumpets carry a central band of yellow the length of each segment, and bright-crimson spots scattered over the white surface. Appareled in noble grace, the lily is as temperamental as it is lovely. Also from Japan, sturdy and dependable in the garden, is the speciosum. Its white flowers are deeply reflexed, almost to the stem, and vividly spotted with rose. Among the several varieties of speciosum one discovers a kind with green streaking; another almost white, so pale are the dots; and the best known, with markings of deep rose, the rubrum. The tiger lily, for many years the only lily grown in home gardens, is easily established. The flowers droop with segments so sharply reflexed that they sometimes overlap at the stem. The color is gorgeous, orange-red or salmon-red with black dots. Among the several lilies often confused with the tiger is the leopard lily, belonging to the United States. The flowers, shaped like those of the tiger, are also bright red, but are spotted with dark crimson. The leopard is extremely hardy in moist soil with partial shade. From Greece comes the scarlet Turk's cap and from Asia another Turk's cap, purple with dark spots. Brilliantly glossy, these caps are splendid against dark shrubbery.

Within the house, lilies show to best advantage in simple arrangements that permit one to enjoy the perfect beauty of the flowers. It is best to remove the anthers from the stamens before arranging. They are usually heavy and so vividly colored that they destroy the purity of the design. Scattered pollen gives a stained effect.

LILY: VARIEGATED

The beauty of lilies makes them appropriate for expressions of romantic extravagance. In this sea fantasy the auratum lilies are the only tangible elements of earthly reality. Sea fans colored to meet the gold stripe of the trumpets build a bold background for crags of coral and strewn sea shells. Plump fishes, rich and strange, nuzzle in the pockets of the coral, flirting their gaudy tails in impish protest at the limits of their little world built within the confines of a bamboo mat.

Lily: Variegated

Lily and Curculigo Capitulata

Lily of the Valley

Most Americans know the lily of the valley as a florist's flower obtainable at any season. To make this steady succession possible the pips are kept in cold storage. As needed, they are removed from refrigeration, planted in greenhouses, and forced into bloom: a process that can be completed in approximately a month if properly done by specialists. The lily is native in Europe, growing wild in many of the wooded regions. The raising of rootstock for export was long a staple industry in Germany, which supplied most of the pips for all countries.

In America the lily of the valley is found wild through the high areas of the Allegheny region. It is very hardy, living easily in gardens where the conditions please it. Because it is a shade-loving plant, it produces its best flowers in a location that at least simulates woodland: under trees, around shrubbery, or in corners of porches. Here it will demand no particular attention if the soil is moderately rich. If it must be planted in the open, set it in a very moist soil that is conditioned once a year with manure and compost. Where it is developed in large beds, it makes a beautiful ground cover during the spring and summer. The heavy mats of creeping rootstock underground and the closely massed foliage among the flowers prevent the intrusion of weeds. Were it an evergreen it would be a year-around satisfaction. Like all lilies, the plant disappears soon after the end of the blooming season.

The "valley," as its friends affectionately call it, is exquisitely refined. Each stalk, set within two pale-green ovate leaves, holds a slender cluster of tiny white nodding bells appropriate for small, delicate designs. The foliage is as valuable as the flowers; lovely in color and form, it is choice combining material.

Lily of the Valley

Lily of the Valley and Azalea

LILY OF THE VALLEY

An analogous color harmony is presented in this arrangement. Sprays of blue forget-me-nots form the lateral placements, small clusters of orchid hydrangeas mass loosely in the center, and half-opened Cecile Brunner roses complete the color sequence. Racemes of lily of the valley liberally spaced to display their airy daintiness head the design. Their white is carried into the center of the pattern through the use of white azaleas. The container is a brilliant piece of modern glass keyed to the smartness of this little miniature.

Magnolia

THE MOST distinctive living things are infrequent and isolated; they must be bought with time and distance. The great redwoods, the saguaro, the Monterey pine are wonders that one travels across the spaces of earth to view; whoever wishes to see them must go to the one small area of their choice. Superlative pronouncements are dangerous; but certainly no one can look upon a magnolia without a realization that he is viewing one of the splendid trees that flower. Nature has been kind to the world in the wide scattering of this beautiful tree, permitting it to live and flourish from North America down through Central America to the West Indies; across broad areas of the Asiatic continent. Wherever it grows, it is a conspicuously noble tree.

The magnolia is built on the grand scale. Several types reach one hundred feet, but because of its spread one does not think in terms of height. The leaves are in scale to the branches, six to ten inches long, oval, and richly glossy. If the foliage is the tree's first claim to beauty, certainly the flowers complete the design. The blossoms are white, infrequently yellow or pink or purple; but it is the creamy white magnolia that one never forgets, viewing it from a slight distance lest one inadvertently touch. For the velvet-textured petals bruise with slightest fingering, and every bruise makes a discolored spot. One easily sees the cupped beauties, because the tree usually stands alone or as stately border for broad avenues.

For arrangements the material should be cut as the bud begins to open. Lay the branch in water, entirely covered, to condition the flower for keeping. With wet fingers gently open the damp bud, folding back the petals to show the full blossom. If both hands and bud are moist, the petals will not stain. At best the whiteness is transient, giving way to beige and brown; but even after the corolla has darkened it is still beautiful in arrangements.

Magnolia

MAGNOLIA

Perfection of floral beauty found in the magnolia is expressed by the balanced symmetry of this design. In floral art balance is usually understood to mean a similarity of lateral placements. In this arrangement the principle is executed in a vertical direction. From the fully opened blossoms at the center the line moves in reversed curves through the opening cups to the light buds. The severe container of dark Japanese pottery is handsome; but in its restraint it offers no competition to the flowers.

Marigold

THE FOLK world has pointed its sprightly jests at the marigold. The name first appears in England, where in Shakespeare's day the marigold lent its pungence to soups and stews, and as kitchen herb was known as pot marigold. This flower is our calendula, grown in warm areas chiefly for gay winter bloom, though it can be brought into flower the year around. New varieties show innumerable color steps from creamy yellow to deep orange.

The marigolds of today are the trinkets of a droll geographical legerdemain. The common marigold of old American gardens is called African marigold, since, before its Mexican origin was established, it was thought to be from Africa. It makes a bushy growth about two feet high with finely cut, pleasantly acrid foliage. The flowers are large, two to four inches across, often with quilled petals. The French marigold, also a native of Mexico, is a much smaller plant, branched near the base yet neat and compact. The flowers range from pure yellow to near-red, with petals usually two-toned in a yellow and red combination. Both the Mexican marigolds are excellent garden material. While the loose-spreading Africans do well in a mixed border or as single plants, the French are used for bedding, and the dwarf variety even as edging. These two marigolds botanically are tagetes.

The Cape marigold—this one truly African—is one to two feet tall, exceedingly varied in type. The tall kind has flat ray flowers, the upper side silver-white with dark-blue center, and the lower side steel-blue. The low plants are very showy, the top of the petals white, yellow, or orange, with the lower side violet to deep purple. The Cape marigold flowers either summer or winter in mild regions. It is a dimorphotheca.

Marigolds are suited to the patterns appropriate for daisies or asters. They need no conditioning beyond the removal of all foliage below the water level.

Marigold

Marigold and Leaves

MARIGOLD

This is a gay, glad design full of sparkle. The container is modern pottery, vividly green, highly glazed, that captures every ray of light in pinpoints of brilliance. Blades of sansevieria shaped into a column the width of the urn offer the one substantial line of the arrangement. Marigolds clustered loosely and in seeming carelessness form the center of the pattern, terminated at the three points by long sprays of Peruvian lilies. The final placement is the brownish-green fruit of a palm tree.

Mondo

E ARE predisposed to think of beauty in terms of size. We glorify the magnificent; we laud the spectacular. Beauty just as truly can be present in small things, although too frequently it passes unnoticed because the minute cannot flaunt itself in eye-stopping gesture. Miniature arrangements of very tiny plant growths can be made in the same patterns that we use for flowers of normal size. By this means we can display the delicate beauty of blossoms too diminutive to appear in the usual designs.

Mondo is a small, pleasant lily, growing freely in many parts of the United States, whose name until recently was ophiopogon. A lover of shade and moisture, it makes a cool, soft ground cover under wide trees. The evergreen foliage is fine, much like grass but thicker, in clumps rising from a dense underground mat of roots. The tiny flowers, close set in racemes about three inches long, range from white through the tints and shades of blue. If planted in open sunlight, mondo displays leaves variegated with a white stripe. Another lily so similar to mondo that only botanists can distinguish between them is liriope; it is, however, more tender than mondo.

Other small lilies make good miniature arrangements. The grape hyacinth is one of the earliest flowers to show through the ground in spring. It is a pretty edging plant. In places where it has escaped from garden control it grows in long drifting rows at the margins of fields like strings of shining blue beads among the grass.

For combining material use single flowers removed from their clustered positions on the stem. Individual blossoms from an agapanthus umbel, one floret of the oleander or the hybrid hydrangea, will adroitly complement the lily. Fine foliage of the lilies themselves will supply greenery, or partly defoliated small sprigs of such shrubs as the eugenia or the myrtle.

Mondo

Mondo with Small Flowers

MONDO

This miniature is prepared to fill a tiny space where the height of the arrangement can be no more than a few inches. The center is filled with small pieces of Queen Anne's lace flanked with the tiniest of Peruvian lilies. Delicate racemes of mondo fan out from the base in the same looseness with which they grow. Because the mondo is the darkest material of the design and has been encouraged to occupy a generous space, it becomes more important than its finely slender proportions would seem to predicate.

NASTURTIUM

This design suggests the dramatic possibilities inherent in the simplest of everyday surroundings. Nasturtiums are supported by yellow marguerites and dried barley. A novel feature is the use of the handsome beards in the main line opposed to the diagonal thrust of the bare stems from which the beards have been removed. The relative position of the nasturtiums and marguerites has been reversed in the two containers to bring the nasturtiums into line. Then the red of the rooster's comb between the two red masses resolves them into a single unit of great importance.

[2 1 9]

Nasturtium

IF ONE mentions South American plants, immediately we think of the tropics. Endlessly we admire orchids, anthuriums, bougainvilleas, cannas, and a host of other beauties; we nourish them in greenhouses or consult their whimseys for garden planting. The broad, splendid tracts of South America outside the hot, moist tropics also have their flowers. The nasturtium has been a part of northern gardens for so many generations that its foreign origin has been long forgotten. Native of the cooler sections of the southern continent, the nasturtium unmistakably is South American. It was Europeanized early in the seventeenth century. There the frugal housewives discovered its food potential: the young pods and seeds they converted into pickles; the gentle piquancy of the leaves and stems enlivened their salads.

In the United States the nasturtiums lead a gay, glad existence, thriving almost anywhere. Start them in warm, moist places. If the soil is rich, or if the plot is shaded, the plants will expand lavishly, pushing out long stems and quantities of enormous leaves but very few flowers. The blossoms are showy in a long scale of yellows, reds, and orange from pale values to heavy tones. Some of the delicate lemon-colored blooms have thin petals almost paperlike in texture, while the maroons and the mahogany shades are lustrous in the sunlight. Though most species produce spotted or striped flowers, there are enough beautiful solid colors to steady the pattern. Double varieties developed recently are as easy to grow as the singles; the difficulty is that many do not produce seeds, and others revert.

Left to their own devices, nasturtiums will ramble blithely through most of the garden, reseeding themselves as they go and appearing in the most surprising places. The tall ones climb trellises and fences, wind around posts or anything that their juicy stems can grasp. They make brilliant informal arrangements. Should combining material be used, let it be sufficiently simple to offer no competition to the flowers.

Nasturtium

Nasturtium and Leaves

Oleander

THE OLEANDER is an evergreen shrub of varied use. Because it endures dust, heat, and wind, it plants well in informal hedges or sidewalk and boulevard trim, besides being an always popular garden ornament. Originally from the Mediterranean, the oleander likes sunshine. It prefers a sandy soil, with well-spaced, thorough waterings during the blooming season. The flowering period is long and so heavy that the shrub must be rested; therefore restore vitality by discontinuing the water or applying it infrequently when the flowers are gone. In the north the oleander is decorative as a tubbed specimen. In pot or in the ground it grows rapidly but accepts heavy pruning; it can, therefore, be kept to any shape or size. Unpruned, it will grow tall yet still maintain its shrubby habit. One plant, then, can produce sufficient color for accent in the small town-garden.

The oleander known to all is the rose-colored double. New varieties recently hybridized cover a wider color range: reds, white, ivory, deep fuchsia, salmon, pink, and coral. Some of these are doubles, most are singles, but all are generously pictorial in landscape effects, amenable to any culture. The oleander will persevere even through almost complete neglect. For best results, however, it needs a certain amount of care beyond irrigation. Above all else, it must be watched for scale insects. Frequent spraying is almost always necessary.

The oleander is easily prepared for arrangements. Remove the leaves. Growing foliage is attractive; the smooth, lance-shaped leaves afford a pleasantly green relief to the masses of color, but they are too thick and leathery to shape readily into floral design. If the arrangement is to be kept several days, immerse the cuttings in very deep water until the petals become crisp. Arranged alone, the showy clusters are tasteful against the bare branches. For more profuse effect fill the spaces with harmonizing material.

OLEANDER

Oleander branches have been divested of their foliage to show the luxuri-
ance of their floral growth. In horizontal arrangements of low, flat design
the two placements should differ slightly in length and in their angle of
deviation from the pure horizontal. The drooping blossom provides variety
in one lateral, as do the open sprays of buds in the opposite line. The large
mass of dark castor bean leaves is not too heavy for this pattern; the fingers
are too narrow, too diverse in their tendencies to seem ponderous.

Oleander

Oleander and Pentstemon

Palm

THE WORLD prizes the palm tree: the tropics value it for economic reasons, the temperate zones for its beauty. Unquestionably the palm is picturesque: a tall trunk mounting for scores of feet without a branch, an umbrella of huge leaves. When one first sees the palm, its sculptured forms impart a feeling of adventitious drama. The foliage gives the tree its distinctive character. Whether the plant is a feather palm, like the date, or a fan palm, it is unlike any other tree. Always it is ornamental, else there would be no long avenues set to palms, where one drives for miles between two rows of straight trunks. Sometimes the trunks are primly smooth, the old leaves removed, the cut edges tidied. More often the ends of the stalks remain, the sawed remnants looking like huge scales of some tremendous cone; or the old leaves from forgotten years still cling to the wood, each layer overlapping those of the years before. Some palms are equipped with thorns on the trunk, even on the leaves, that make painful wounds. Many of the thorns are so irritating that they are used in blowpipes by South American Indians to do the work of poisoned arrows. One learns to avoid palm thorns.

Apart from street and highway planting, the palm is grown extensively in gardens. The one requirement is abundant water. Even the fan palm indigenous to hot southwestern sections of the United States thrives lustily only if well supplied with moisture. The most famous palms in this area are unplanted, native growth; but, though in desert country, they live in a narrow canyon fed by a small mountain stream.

The palm leaf is most useful for spectacular design. Employed alone, it can be shaped into fine patterns of light and shade; through its simplicity it affords strong backing for brilliant flowers, especially those of tropical nature. Should it start to fold up, immerse it flat in water.

Palm

Palm and Eucalyptus

PALM

Precise placement has wrought spreading palm fans into a swinging curve
with its implications of slender, sinuous beauty. This effect has been made
possible in part by turning the fronds edgewise and in part by concealing a
portion of the fans so that one is aware chiefly of the receding line of the
lattice. Two strips of palm sheath form the tallest line. The foreground is
filled with one gorgeous torch ginger, fully open, whose color extends to
the top of the design in unopened buds.

Palo Verde

THE GREAT arid stretches of the southwestern United States have an abundant plant life. Gay color in the early spring makes the desert an artist's paradise where one hesitates to step lest a tiny flower be crushed into the sand. The trees that grow sparingly beside the dry washes and sandy stream-beds are always picturesque in shape. Creatures of the wind, they stand in fantastic posture, their arms bent and twisted by the force of the blown sand.

By desert standards the palo verde is large. Twenty or so feet high and wide-spreading, it crowns the highlands beside the empty washes. On the ground beneath it is usually a heap of broken and dead branches, unless they have been swept away in one of the flash floods that carve new ways for the streams. The tree is drought-resistant and makes excellent use of any available water. Beautiful in spring, with its green trunk and bright-yellow flowers, it is also handsome after the foliage has disappeared and the shadowy network of the branches stands alone.

The smoke tree is even more lovely than the palo verde. It is not so resistant as its cousin; its great need of water leads it to the bottom of the washes, where it waits the coming of the floods and all too often is destroyed. During its short life it gives its full measure of beauty. The fine branches are almost entirely without foliage, but in late spring the whole shrub bursts into sudden brief flower with clouds of blue-violet blossoms against the gray-green wood. It looks like a lovely violet mist floated from the sky.

Another tree found along the washes is the desert ironwood, also wide-spreading. It blooms at the same time as the smoke tree, with darker flowers of violet-purple showing among the green leaves that make a brief appearance.

All this desert growth works easily into dried arrangements.

PALO VERDE

Holiday arrangements can be delicate. This design has all the sparkle of
the Christmas season but nothing of the conventional coloring, none of
the profuse foliage effects associated with the winter. A branch of the palo
verde tree, its fine twigs showing like a network of mist, stands beside a
piece of silvered brush whose branches are topped by Christmas tree ornaments. Skeletonized magnolia leaves form a background diaphanous as
cloud stuff against which the reindeer are placed.

Palo Verde

Palo Verde with Accessories

Pandanus

Had Robinson Crusoe been cast upon a shore lined with pandanus trees, he could have solved the problems of existence so immediately that Defoe's chief difficulty would have been the extension of his story to book length. In its native tropics the pandanus makes a tall, unbranched tree with huge clusters of long, slender leaves growing in great, spiraling terminals from the few outgrowths at the top. To support this unstable crown, aerial roots extend as props from the trunk to the ground. The fruit is a heavy cone with scores of small, angular phalanges that are bright, glossy green on the outside and an equally vivid orange at their base. The growing habits of the leaves and the fruit give the tree its common name of screw pine. The entire tree is useful: the roots supply fiber for ropes and nets; the leaves are braided and woven into hats, baskets, and mats for floor coverings; the fruit is edible.

Outside the tropics the pandanus can be established as a handsome potted plant in the moist warmth of the greenhouse. The species most suitable for house plant and for floral arrangements has leaves two to three feet long and two or three inches wide variegated with bands of white or silver striping. A more ordinary variety is green without markings.

Another tropical foliage plant similar in culture is the cordyline. It is called dracæna by florists and ti in the Pacific islands. Though it is not a dracæna, it is close kin. The leaves are exceedingly graceful and variously colored: vivid green, dark metallic red, bronze-purple, even pink and white. The venation of these leaves, approximating embossment, is a very real part of their beauty. Often the midribs are bright red.

Such foliage material is most effective alone in severe design, so arranged that the play of light upon the leaves reveals their textured beauty. The leaves will keep for months.

Pandanus

Pandanus and Agapanthus

PANDANUS

Tropical as the South Seas themselves, these materials are set in a basket of braided pandanus fiber. Leaves of the striped pandanus, their tops slashed in smart diagonals to parallel the edges of the basket, stand erect in the center. Brilliant hibiscus blossoms threaded on coco rib occupy a conspicuous position in the foreground, balanced on the other side of the design by a lei of red carnations. Bananas and the heavy cone of the pandanus fruit complete the design.

Pelargonium

THE SHOW or fancy pelargonium is grown today more extensively and more successfully than at any earlier portion of this twentieth century. As its common name implies, it is an old American favorite re-established in popular taste, for we call it the Lady Washington geranium. Its ancestry goes far beyond the Revolutionary period. This beautifully marked flower so delighted the first Englishmen to see it in its native South Africa that it was introduced into England in the seventeenth century, even sooner than the ancestors of our common geraniums. Many flower growers experimented almost exclusively with this aristocrat of the geranium tribe. Before any pelargonium had been developed to the hardiness necessary for existence as bedding material, this show plant was a successful greenhouse inhabitant.

The Lady Washington pelargonium usually is treated as a specimen plant, sometimes set in the perennial border. It is not so generally grown as the zonal because it is more difficult. It does not enjoy hot summers and has a much shorter blooming period than do the ordinary varieties. After it has stopped flowering, it should be given a rest period before being cut back. During the winter it requires only sparing irrigation. In the very early spring, when vigorous growth begins, it usually needs food. With the best of care the life of the Lady Washington is rather brief. But the exceptional beauty of the blossoms repays all one's vigilant efforts.

Not in any sense of the word is this a common flower. It is large and exquisitely colored, with markings often deeper in tone than the basic hue. In shape and coloring it so much resembles the azalea that it can be substituted for the azalea without in any way debasing the tone of the arrangement. The pelargonium picked in bud stage needs deep immersion for conditioning.

Pelargonium

Pelargonium and Ivy

PELARGONIUM

The innate elegance of the pelargonium makes possible this studied pattern. A rich Satsuma vase has been used to correspond with the other materials but is largely concealed in the design so that it will not overpower the blossoms. Pelargonium blooms and pink roses form a slender tower surmounted by a cluster of pink ostrich tips that extend down one side, ending in a fluffy mass on the table. The flowers are set close together, though not crowded; the loose spacing of informal or naturalistic arrangement would be inappropriate with these accessories.

PEONY

Richness of color characterizes this design fashioned of brilliant flowering
material. Tall spires of larkspur mark the outlines of the arrangement. The
fine tips of unopened buds that terminate most of the stalks, and the consistent irregularity of stem lengths within a placement to produce interesting spaces, contribute to the beauty of the pattern. Against the purple of
the larkspur the deep rose of the peonies creates a warm glow that extends
to all parts of the arrangement.

Peony

MANY of our choicest plants originated in Asia. From China, in particular, come some of our loveliest. For centuries before its introduction into western Europe the Chinese cultivated the peony, that aristocrat of the buttercup family. Like many a human member of the privileged classes it lives easily and graciously in an environment suited to its taste. Though it prefers a rich soil in full sun, clay loam well drained but moist, it accepts partial shade. Light protection from direct sunlight protects the flowers from a too rapid fading. But not any canopy will do, not large trees since the peony resents the intrusion of heavy roots into its ground area. Cold weather does not disturb the peony; it insists on complete winter rest, possible only in chilly temperatures. For that reason it is not successful in semi-tropical belts, whose temperate winters make a real dormancy almost impossible. Once established, the peony does not wish to be moved. Since it should be left undisturbed for many years, it must be located carefully with space for full development. In the large garden, where it belongs rather than in the small town-lot, it does not dwarf its neighbors with its masses of bloom. Situated thus to its liking, the peony is exceedingly hardy.

The beauty of the peony is as notable as its hardiness. The colors are varied and attractive with exquisite combinations of hues occurring in the doubles: clear white with rose center, deep rose with silver-edged corolla, yellow-tinged blossoms. If other material is combined with the peony, it should have sufficient refinement to justify its inclusion. With such flowers as the camellia, the delphinium, the tuberose, the small lily, one can devise deft color harmonies, yet maintain the general elegance of the whole. The blossoms will last a week or more if picked in tight-bud stage, then almost completely defoliated.

Peony

Peony and Aspidistra

Peruvian Lily

FLORAL designers enjoy working with the lily, for it so patently is one of the garden elite. If its size compels other choice, the arranger may select from the small lilylike flowers. The Peruvian lily is an amaryllis, usually a greenhouse plant, but in warm areas quite at home in the garden. It needs rich soil in partial shade with liberal irrigation. Even where the temperature permits winter existence it should be lifted, if for no other reason than to divide the tubers, since they increase more rapidly than one location will support. The plant makes a sightly accent against shrubbery with its slender, lance-shaped leaves, often twisted at the base. The flowers are diversely colored, some entirely yellow, a particularly vibrant tone; a few green-tipped or spotted. Another kind whose fringed leaves are bluish green has rose-colored blossoms. One dark beauty is resplendently red, with brown or purple spots and green tips.

The Peruvian lily is a summer bloomer. Late winter and early spring offer abundant choice. Two other amaryllises are the twin snowdrop and snowflake. Their tiny, nodding bells, white and green, will grow under trees or shrubbery for years, happy if undisturbed. The Chilean glory of the sun only recently introduced into the United States is a true lily. It is exquisitely blue, translucent as if made of porcelain. Three small irises, all from South Africa, can be given the same care as the freesia, also an iris and likewise from Africa. The first one, the babania, grows in loose clusters of tiny but showy flowers in red, lilac, or blue; the brilliant ixia, most popular of the group, lasts for days in the sunshine along with its close relative, the sparaxis, or wandflower, whose brightness ends the spring and advances into summer.

These flowers keep well in arrangements if set in shallow water.

PERUVIAN LILY

A very close shading of color values with subtle variations in hue induces a refinement that is difficult to secure by other means, and yet is very charming in contemporary rooms of brilliant simplicity. Long sprays of Peruvian lilies are paralleled with plumes of yellow celosia whose sheen enhances the delicate luster of the small lilies. Tawny red blossoms of the trumpet vine complete the design. The red is used sparely; except for the basal cluster, only a few trumpets are introduced among the sprays, enough to unify the design.

Peruvian Lily

Peruvian Lily and Gerbera

Petunia

ETUNIAS originated in the southern portions of South America, especially Argentina, with one or two varieties from Mexico. Not only do they belong to the tobacco family, but their name is said to have been derived from an aboriginal South American term for tobacco. The common garden petunia is a low plant of straggling growth usually treated as a tender annual. Not particular about its soil, it will flower profusely on rich land; yet some of the most attractive bedding petunias make excellent covers in poor soil if given enough moisture. Either sun or partial shade is acceptable, though sun for at least half the day is desirable.

The plant is difficult to handle. The stems are weak, and the leaves are soft and flabby. All portions of the plant are sticky, yet brittle. Weeding petunias demands meticulous effort to avoid breaking off portions of the trailing stalks or dislodging the blossoms, which fit very loosely inside their sheaths. But the beauty of the flowers is sufficient reward for the trouble. The corolla is funnel-shaped, broad and open at the mouth, sometimes four and five inches or more across in the large varieties, with petal edges fringed or fluted or ruffled, falling away from the mouth in fat, round curves. These giants come in deep, rich tones of rose and red and purple; some in solid colors, others veined or streaked. Massed against shrubbery at the front of the border, they give a finely decorative finish. The small types, those called bedding or balcony petunias, are very sprawling, with small, clean-lined flowers. They are used for formal beds and for edgings or undergrowth; it is these bright plants whose pendent habits make window boxes and hanging baskets.

Petunias are best arranged in their natural lines of growth in broad, horizontal lines; or they may appear as rich accent against inconspicuous accessory material.

Petunia

PETUNIA

Pendent grace of flowers that trail lovely ground covers is revealed in this study of petunias. While establishing a strong base, a cluster of deep-rose blossoms displays one of the fine points of the design, two flowers that dip their curling rims over the edge of the container. Long sprays in pale rose and in white streaked with the same hue extend the dominant color and the pendulous position throughout the design. Skeletonized avocado leaves build a tenuous edging, their frail tips pointing the lines of the pattern.

Pine

THE MOST valuable tree of the north temperate zone is the pine. For practical economic virtues no other conifer can approach it. Though not the most beautiful, for some of the firs and spruces are more shapely and more attractively colored, it is quite ornamental enough, and undeniably it is a friendly tree. One loves the pine, even as the spreading oaks, with a companionable affection; the pine is a tree with which to live. It will adjust to many locations other than the highlands to which it belongs, if it is provided with some of the conditions found on its hilltops: it must have good drainage to approximate the run-off from a mountain; and its crown must sway freely in light and air. Therefore it almost always overtops its neighbors in its urgent search for isolation. Yet both winter and summer it needs protection from hot, dry winds. Winter or summer it desires shelter. The young pine uses all the vigor and plasticity of its youth to erect a shapely pyramid around its trunk or central column, which rises from the ground to its head. From this trunk at regular intervals the branches radiate in whorls, an especially flattering style for a pyramid. In middle years difficult living conditions, sudden changes of temperature, harsh winds probably have made it scraggly in its midlength. But when it has attained old age and topped its neighbors, the vigor that sustained it to full height and brought it out to free air completes its growth with a tip as shapely as the young tree of years before.

The pine is adaptable for arrangements. It can be used in the Oriental manner, very simply with spare lines. As background for flowers, particularly those which grow under trees, it creates an illusion of cool woods pleasing for the hot days of summer. Or it invites rich ornamentation for the Christmas season.

Pine

Pine and Rhododendron

PINE

This arrangement depicts the persistence of life. A forest giant endeavoring to recover vigor through new growth is represented by a warped fragment of wood, weathered and seamed from long exposure. The wooden board suggests earth. Rocks, common on hilltops, conceal water holders. On the pine branch fresh tips and a cluster of young, soft cones pledge a hale and verdant future. Delicate teardrop moss counterfeits the lichens natural to the location, and the tiny figure of the old man portrays longevity.

PITCHER PLANT

Singular plants should be arranged to display their odd characteristics. Tall leafstalks show on some the face, on others the reverse of the pitcher. At the base is a cluster of blossoms like fairy umbrellas sheltering some elfin assembly. The odd coloring unifies the design, tones that hint the dankness of the saturated earth from which the plants were cut. Chartreuse recurs in the container; blue-green of some stems and flowers is intensified by folded canna leaves whose red tones match the spots on the pitcher plant.

Pitcher Plant

Some of the most interesting plants grow in unsightly places. Out of the bogs and marshes in the eastern United States come the pitcher plants. Because they grow wild in locations difficult of access, few people see them in their native surroundings. The tender varieties can be nurtured in greenhouses, but many grow in gardens simulating their wild environment. They need black, sandy soil, peat, or sphagnum moss, which must be kept moist.

The entire plant is curious in appearance, beautiful in its strangeness. The leaves can easily be mistaken for flowers. In the spring three to eight stalks grow from the base of the plant, each topped with a single leaf; sometimes a second set appears in the fall. Each leaf is shaped like a pitcher partially tipped to pour, with a flexible lip that, in the carnivorous varieties, forms a lid to close the opening after the insects have entered. The foliage is usually pale green with purplish or white spots, and often is conspicuously veined. One of the tall types whose ancestors are said to have lived in the garden of Charles I of England has pitchers shaded from dark green to purple, with fine hairs on the inside of the lid. The flower is as odd as the leaf, repeating part, sometimes all, of the coloring on the pitcher. The most interesting detail is the stigma on the pistil, which is almost as large as the width of the flower; bent down all around, it looks like a plump toadstool huddling among the petals.

Immerse all the plant parts in water before arranging. The stem holds a great deal of water. If it is filled, the arrangement will keep. Should one be so fortunate as to have stems, leaves, and flowers together with bits of marsh grass, a realistic design is delightful. The oddly shaped leaves used alone can be wrought into remarkable abstractions.

Pitcher Plant

Plum

STONE fruits bear delicately lovely flowers. Typical of spring in the freshness of early bloom, they have appeared infrequently in flower arrangements because each severed branch decreases the yield of fruit. The ornamental species may be cut without compunction. Although many so-called flowering trees bear fruit, it is usually small and tasteless. Most gardens have room for at least one tree. In large landscapes planted to avenues of bloom, the flowering fruits have few rivals. Winding parkway borders canopied by their fragile masses of color create a beauty as gentle as it is fleeting. For the period of bloom is short; the petals slip into the air to shower the ground with the slightest of mosaics.

Though the blossoms are short-lived, the trees are hardy and generally easy to maintain. Probably the best known are the cherry and the peach. The Japanese flowering cherries are exceptionally attractive. The blossoms are usually white, some palest pink; many are single, a few almost as large as small roses. The flowering peach is brilliantly pink. The tall, rather slender tree with heavy clusters of double-flowered blossoms affords material for vivid display. Dark branches, bare of leaves but glowing with color, will brighten any room. Not so well known as the peach but similar in effect is the flowering almond, whose pink is clearer than the deep rose of the peach.

Perhaps a more lasting satisfaction for the floral designer comes from the flowering plum. It, too, has lovely blossoms of purest white. But the tree itself, with its purple-red foliage, is a handsome addition to any garden. The leaves of most flowering trees are inconsequential for floral design, but the deep and shining richness of the plum lasts through the autumn. Neat in form, thin and delicately textured, the foliage is beautiful alone or makes a mellow background for light combining material. Total immersion of leaves ensures lasting satisfaction.

PLUM

The ripeness of color that distinguishes the Japanese flowering plum is unusual in the temperate zone. The warm red-browns are almost exactly repeated in the leaves of the red canna. Two placements of plum foliage are supported by canna blades to extend the overly slender trunk area. Folded leaves low within the container carry the dominant tone through the green of the bells of Ireland. One twig of ripened fruit adds a glowing color accent.

Plum

Plum and Castor Bean

Princess Flower

Tropical South America has more than two hundred species of the shrub tibouchina, yet only two or three kinds are known in the United States, and only one type is widely grown. That one is so beautiful that it has been given the name of glory bush or princess flower. The amazing stamens have caused some people to call it the spider flower. For greenhouse adornment it would be hard to find a handsomer plant. In warm belts where it will grow outdoors, it is a favorite for its spectacular inflorescence.

In some locations the princess flower can be developed into a bushy shrub; but where the environment is entirely to its liking it makes an open, leggy growth as much as ten feet tall. It must be protected from the wind, for the long stalks will snap all too easily. It does not like much direct sunlight. If planted where it has plenty of air circulation, yet is protected somewhat by taller shrubs, it will thrive. The leaves are large and oval, so closely covered with fine hairs on the upper surface that they feel furry to the touch. The venation is one of the most conspicuous features of the leaf. From three to seven veins run the length, interlocked with side veins. The main ribs are deeply depressed, making the foliage seem to spring sharply from the stem. The flower buds, growing in small, scattered clusters, are as hairy as the leaves, bright pink and rounded like awkward, misformed balls. They open to show flowers three or more inches across, a glowing royal purple.

The blooming period is very long, but each flower lasts only one day, even less in active wind. Pick when the buds are closed, before they begin to show color; then immerse completely in water. Only by this conditioning will the flowers stand in the arrangement.

Princess Flower

Princess Flower and Clover

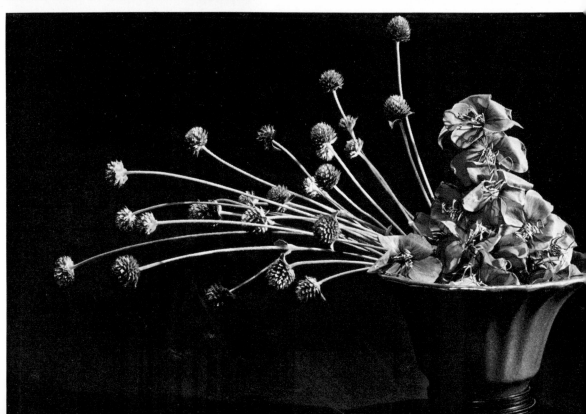

PRINCESS FLOWER

Resplendent reds and royal purple make a gorgeous combination. Three stalks of gladioli build a brilliant vertical support for the princess flowers, whose several sprays form a sketchy horizontal triangle. A fuchsia that combines the purple of the princess flower and the red of the gladiolus showers its blossoms in airy profusion to extend the base of the design to a width comparable with the height. The clear blue of the container is a daring color accent in this tonal scheme.

Privet

A HEDGE can be a beautiful unit of landscape design. More gracious than a fence for the property-dividing line between small gardens, more intimate than a wall for the separation of unrelated areas within a large garden, it is either informal or dignified to fit the setting. Most popular of all hedge plants is the privet, a shrub—sometimes a tree—of the olive family. Its unusual adaptability ensures its success in the garden. It will grow in any ordinary soil; and though it likes sun and will stand dryness, it lives almost equally well in shade, even under trees where it endures dripping moisture. It is not discouraged by the smoke of city streets, the dust of open fields, nor the winds along the coast.

Among the privets are both deciduous and evergreen varieties. The kind most used for hedges, though called California privet, is really native to Japan. It is a half evergreen shrub of stiffly erect habits, with neat, small leaves that are dark green and shining on the upper surface. It can be kept pruned to any height, however low, and will stand the severe cutting of a formal hedge; but it grows so rapidly that the frequent shearing necessary to maintain the architectural lines prevents the development of flowers. This privet will reach a height of fifteen feet if left to its own devices. When one wants an informal screen, the loose, unclipped branches are attractive in early summer, with their slender terminal spikes of tiny white flowers and the small dark berries that remain long on the stems, sometimes most of the winter. Though the plain green variety is most enduring for hedges, some of the others are more handsome, especially those with large leaves variegated in yellow or white.

Privet needs only deep immersion for conditioning. Then it will last a long time. Any design created in privet is suitable for all small-leaved branches without flowers.

Privet

Privet and Chrysanthemums

PRIVET

Verticals with fringed edges can be either unpleasantly careless and slip-
shod or delightfully informal. The delicate grace of this material is accentu-
ated by the irregularity of tips of the branching privet. Variegated privet
should be used in a design as high in key as this tonal scheme. The green
centers of the leaves, so lightly echoed in the pendent grapes, is a charming frame for the orchid gladioli. A black urn with gold motifs lends stable
dignity to the arrangement.

Pyracantha

MONG the shrubs popular for autumn and winter arrangements
the pyracantha holds high place. Native of remote areas in southeastern
Europe and on through Asia into central China and the Himalayan region,
it long has been established in the United States. It is a half-evergreen
shrub, usually small, though under the most favorable circumstances some
plants will reach fifteen feet. If given a comfortable, warm position in the
sun, it will adapt itself to any soil. It forms very dense, impenetrable hedges
or covers for walls and fences, since it can be sharply pruned to height.
Scattered plants make attractive hillside growth, where they shape themselves to the slope of the ground. In a border for background planting the
tall varieties of pyracantha give bright accent in autumn and winter.

Most kinds are stiff, rather angular in branching habits, as opposed
to the wide arches of the cotoneaster. The foliage is fine and bright, the
small, narrow leaves attached to the stalk by the shortest of stems. In early
summer tiny white flowers appear in many-branched clusters, followed by
minute berries, pale green when they first appear, changing their color as
they increase in size and ripen. By early fall the fruit is mature. The slender
branches then are almost completely covered with bright red or orange,
brilliant colors that, together with a liberal supply of fierce thorns, give
the shrub its common name of firethorn.

The pyracantha makes shapely floral designs. Completely defoliate
the branches to emphasize the berries. Larger and much brighter than
cotoneaster berries, they are the principal feature in the arrangement. Cut
the stem horizontally, then slash vertically to encourage the water to rise.
Always remove the thorns, since they make painful scratches or puncture
wounds. The branches are pliant enough to be bent or curved into any desired shape. The arrangement will last well.

Pyracantha

Pyracantha and Celosia

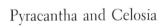

PYRACANTHA

Placed in a brass compote that expresses the lowest tone of the color scheme, pyracantha is shaped into reiterative curves. Within the only completed loop, small plumes of yellow celosia follow the highest placement, and dip over the edge of the compote to form the two limits of a bright cluster of yellow baby chrysanthemums. An example of selective discrimination is shown in the bare branch of the central loop; denuded of most of its berries, it emphasizes the colorful placement it encircles.

Queen Anne's Lace

Common fare of the old-fashioned kitchen depends to an astonishing extent upon the carrot family. Soups, stews, pickles, relishes, salads: all are impossible without the carrot. For from the carrot domain we draw anise and caraway for their tricky flavor; the indispensable dill for pickles and relishes; carrots, of course; parsnips and celery; then parsley to garnish the dish. Nothing of all this is glamorous, nothing to impel one irresistibly to the table; but in the garden patch they grow tall and flower in delicate beauty. They are recognized by their leaves, deeply and repeatedly cut into fine segments that suggest fern. The blossoms stand in flat umbels set in a whorl of bracts resembling leaves.

Queen Anne's lace, the florist's aristocrat of this plebeian tribe, is the wild carrot that riots along any dusty country road in midsummer. It started its lusty career in eastern Europe or Asia; eventually as a weed it made its way into the fields of North America, where it created agricultural dismay. It expends all its energy above ground; the roots are small and unsuitable for food. It was, perhaps, from some common source that both this weed and the vegetable carrot are descended. The first improvement of the carrot seems to have been made in Holland; later it appeared in England to add fresh savor to Tudor tables. The vegetable heads are lovely, but not so exquisitely lacelike as the weed.

Australia has a blue laceflower popular as a florist's flower in the United States, also grown in many gardens as a tender annual. Only two feet in height, slender and weak-stemmed, it needs staking or the protection of other plants to hold it erect. Now known as trachymene, it formerly was called didiscus and is still sold under the latter name.

Both laceflowers make delicately airy arrangements. Defoliate the stems, immerse deeply, not wetting the flowers, then set loosely in dainty containers.

Queen Anne's Lace

Queen Anne's Lace and Fern

QUEEN ANNE'S LACE

Despite its size this entire composition expresses airy grace. Single flowers of Queen Anne's lace are tiny florets, scarcely discernible one from another in the umbels of dusty white. The heads themselves, irregularly spaced, show frail stems here and there against the background. Three rubrum lilies are fully opened to reveal their rosy dapplings, like the florets of the lace. Their star pattern and two slender buds make the transition in tone to the ruby bowl of the container.

RHODODENDRON

Two rare flowers are combined for their companionable coloring. A branch of the orchid tree has been stripped of all leaves. With flowering sprays left only on the inner side of the curving branch, it makes a neat directional sweep, since the blossoms all point to the cluster of rhododendrons at the foot of the tall placement. The container and floral treatment share equally in the voids and masses.

Rhododendron

IF THIS world ever arrives at a point of agreement with Emerson that "beauty is its own excuse for being," then the rhododendron should be selected as world emblem. It has so few economic virtues to commend it to the woodsman's ax of materialistic civilization that it has been allowed to thrive unmolested and to spread its exceptional beauty through a good part of the cool regions of the world. In the United States it grows through the eastern and the northwestern coastal mountains. It inhabits high altitudes of tropical Asia extending south from the Himalayas to New Guinea and Australia. Asia is the favorite dwelling-place of the rhododendron. More varieties are found in China than anywhere else in the world.

Its cultural desires cannot be satisfied everywhere. The ideal soil is porous, containing enough fibrous material to retain moisture; it is acid with, preferably, a high peat content. The exposure is as important as the soil. Partial shade with protection from wind can be contrived if the rhododendron is planted under trees such as fruit trees or oaks or conifers that root deeply and provide broken rather than deep shade. Intense light seems even more critically disturbing than temperature. Do not cultivate the soil, for the shallow-rooting rhododendron is easily injured; a good mulch will prevent weeds.

Though the shrub can be used alone as a single specimen, it is more attractive set in masses against dark green trees. This planting not only simulates natural growing conditions, but provides proper background for the flowers.

The azalea is related to the rhododendron and requires much the same culture. It needs a little more light. A few species injured by cold succeed in the southern United States.

These flowers are difficult to keep. Pick in bud stage when the lowest flower begins to show color. Defoliate, then immerse the entire branch. They shape into exquisite patterns, needing no accompaniment.

Rhododendron

Rhododendron and Melianthus Major

Rocks

Almost all Oriental art is symbolical. In Japanese gardens every detail means more than meets the eye. Beyond other nations the Orientals use rocks in their landscapes not merely for the picturesque value of the stones but to suggest the latent power of nature; and no effort is too great to achieve the end they have in mind. In one of the public parks of Japan is a huge rock at the edge of a pond; its height is intensified by its mirrored reflection in the water until it looks like a mountain beside a lake. So dramatic is the effect that those who see it silently thank the landscape artist for his skill in contriving a pool under the rock. The designer, however, achieved his effect oppositely. The pool he had. In his search for a suitable rock he found miles away this admirable mountainlike cliff, which he then had blasted into a hundred great pieces. Bit by bit he assembled it in his park so skillfully that with the help of trees and vines the effect of the blasting was concealed. Just as Japanese paintings are full of hidden ideas and subtle suggestions, so can the rocks in their gardens suggest some loved scene. Through shape and position they keep awake the memory of a favorite place.

The Western use of rocks is not symbolic. We use them in our gardens, particularly if we have streams or pools, because we love the sound of water splashing against pebbles. We like moss that drapes tree branches above water and lichens that crowd the cracks between the stones. We like the idea of bright flowers against the grimness of granite or fish tailing their way between small buried boulders. In a small way a clever arrangement can create something of the same feeling. Piles of little rocks have far greater possibilities than a few large ones; they can be shaped and reshaped in endless variety. With bits of tree material, small ferns, and moss one interprets the cool outdoors. To the materialist small stones make prime covering for flower holders, even to color selection, with pink stones, perhaps, used with pink flowers.

ROCKS

A large arrangement of woodland material creates an illusion of forest and
stream. Pieces of flagstones are piled in rocky prominences. From behind
one peak emerges a fully leaved branch of the Japanese maple, shaped to
suggest a mature tree. Long fronds of the woodwardia fern occupy the
front position of greatest prominence; even an unfurled tip of new growth
has been included to heighten the realism. Small ferns and teardrop moss
complete the design.

Rocks.　Rocks with Pine

Rose

HE ROSE is the flower of the world. It lived before records existed; it has been cultivated by almost every civilized people. The modern highly developed rose is more demanding than the sturdy, sweet-scented ones of old gardens. Today's hybrids should be planted by themselves, apart from other flowers, where they can be given the treatment they need. The soil must be dug much deeper than for most plants and well fertilized before the roses are set out. Irrigate only when the ground is dry, but irrigate thoroughly; then cultivate as soon as the surface permits. The tea roses do well only in the southern United States, because they do not like cold weather; yet the hybrid teas are found the country over. Vigorous and hardy, long-blooming, they are thoroughly dependable.

The tea rose has a restricted color range; among the hybrid teas, however, are all the colors as yet possible in roses: clear yellow, golden and apricot and salmon tones, copper tinged with pink, copper flushed with flame—to mention only a few variations of one hue. Recent development has refined the form of the bud until now we have roses with oval tips, tips that taper to a sharp point, tips with flaring edges. Of recent years a widespread demand for climbing roses has compelled hybridizers to develop hardy roses capable of unusually vigorous growth. For there are no true climbers among roses. What we call a climbing rose is not an actual vine but a sturdy rose plant growing definitely upright and producing stalks taller than normal height.

Pick roses in bud stage when they first begin to show color. They fade as soon as they open in sunlight. Remove all thorns and such leaves as will stand below water level. The flowers will open slowly in the container, and their color will be true.

Rose

Rose with Other Flowers

ROSE

A delightful hospitality is extended by these two figurines of beautiful
Venetian glass. The graciousness of their pose is marked by the single rose
within one hand and the tall sprays in the other hand. Unequal in height
and inclined toward each other, the branches belong together as one arrangement. A closer placement would destroy their individuality; even a
slight removal would destroy the unity. No single figure, however charming, could express the mannered welcome of these retainers of a patrician
household.

Sansevieria

THE FIFTY or more species of sansevieria are members of the lily family from Africa and India. In the United States the plant is esteemed for its beautiful foliage. Where the air is consistently warm, it grows easily in the garden, not requiring any particular care if it is set in heavy soil and watered regularly. Farther north it makes an excellent potted specimen for house decoration because it does not require much sunlight or continued fresh air if the leaves are sponged off occasionally.

The foliage is the most important part of the plant for its economic virtues as well as its beauty. The leaves grow in a cluster from the base two to three feet long, slender for their height and very stiff, so hard and resistant to pressure that they feel almost like thin pieces of wood. They look gray-green because they are mottled in unpatterned effect with flecks of pale green. Some varieties are striped transversely with narrow bands of pale green or gray-white. A very slim marginal stripe around the edge, either of dark red or creamy yellow, further accents the leaf form. The flowers are inconspicuous. Borne in dense racemes, they are, for the most part, creamy-white tinged with rose or pale green and supported by bracts of ivory-green. The sansevieria reserves its florescence, unfortunately, for its natural state; very seldom does the plant bloom in cultivation in temperate zones.

It has several pictorial folk names. From the spotted variegation of the leaves it is called snake plant or leopard lily. In its native tropics, where the sansevieria is a source of fiber material, it is known as bowstring hemp.

The sansevieria is invaluable in flower arrangement. Either in shallow water or without water it will last a long time, retaining its heavy, shining gloss. It is sufficiently handsome to stand alone or as patterned background for other material.

SANSEVIERIA

The beauty inherent in marshaled array is manifest in this pattern of exotic plant material. The tight Gothic spire is shaped by dexterous overlapping of the sansevieria blades until the congruence of their edges almost obliterates the separateness of their forms. Two monstera leaves, of the same color value as the sansevieria, but thin against the hard resistance of the blades, establish a placement for the colorful fruit of the pandanus.

Sansevieria

Sansevieria and Anthurium

Spathiphyllum

THE SPATHIPHYLLUM is a tropical American plant related to the anthurium, which it resembles in culture and general appearance. Despite their similarity the two plants require different conditioning and treatment. Since the spathiphyllum wilts easily, it must be immersed completely, then set in a deep-water container. The anthurium is not immersed; its container holds shallow water.

At home the spathiphyllum grows in shade with a great deal of moisture, almost in mud. It needs tight planting with closely matted roots; consequently it cannot be transplanted. Here it is grown in some warm greenhouses for its beautiful foliage, but with indifferent success. Though the type form is handsome, some of the hybridized varieties are exceedingly beautiful. The material used here is the white spathiphyllum.

The leaves on short leafstalks are long, wide lances with heavy main veins. Thinner than many leaves their size, and flexible, they seem more refined than much of the lush tropical foliage. The upper surface of the spathe is a rich white that suggests the purity of the calla lily; the back of the blade is the same lively green as the stalk. A delicately green vein system on both surfaces of the blade gives a pleasant suggestion of freshness and the cool out-of-doors. As the flower ages, the white upper surface slowly turns green. Since the plant blooms throughout the year, it displays at any time both white and green blades. The scattering fresh growth among the matured and aging spathes produces a delightful tone harmony, since the spathiphyllum is beautiful at all stages. The spadix at first is as white as the spathe, the position of each tiny flower showing like the mere dot of an intricate pattern in filigree. With development these dots gradually change to the green of the spathe back; finally they become the calyxes of minute white flowers covering the spadix.

Spathiphyllum

Spathiphyllum and Strelitzia

SPATHIPHYLLUM

The heliconia is a handsome plant. Large leaves of the bronze variety have been folded down the midrib to establish the long curve that extends almost from table level to the tip of the design. Transverse venation lighter in value than the leaf fiber provides variation of tone. One stalk of the hybrid spathiphyllum seems doubly white against the deep red-brown of the heliconia. The facing spathes, some white, some ivory—and the green of the reversed blades—all are lovely whether bent in soft folds or trimly oval.

Stock

STOCK is indispensable for gardener and florist alike. Because it has been a favorite always, even among our colonial forebears, it has been developed carefully, with particular attention to color and length of bloom. Ranging from white through delicate pinks to deep rose, and from palest lavender to rich purple, it is unusually adaptable for mass effects. The plant is hardy. Though it prefers a sunny location in well-drained, rather sandy loam, it will accept any reasonable cultural environment. Since it is a cool-temperature resident, it produces its finest blossoms in spring and very early summer, even in winter. The period of bloom is long, providing color and attractive fragrance for many weeks.

Heaviness of floral growth is rare in the spikes of ordinary garden plants: the larkspur is dainty; the pentstemon and the snapdragon separate their blossoms; but the profuseness of the stock, with flower crowded against flower, results in a density of color that sometimes looks best when used without other blossoms or foliage. The stem often has excessive leafage, which should be removed, at least in part, the better to display the flowers. With little effort stock can be shaped into beautiful arrangements, preferably patterns of simple outline where generous spacing will show to good advantage the tall racemes of closely massed flowers. Because one thinks of stock only as racemose inflorescence, one seldom looks at the individual florets. Their beauty deserves more attention than they customarily receive. Deeply rounded petals, almost velvety in texture, suggest other flowers, if one desires a combination: violets, pansies, carnations, roses, or lilies, each in its season.

Freshly cut stock wilts because the semi-woody stem draws water slowly. If cut back into the softer wood, the stalk can be conditioned in deep water for lasting arrangements.

Stock

Stock and Cabbage

STOCK

Flowers and vegetables handsome in color or strong in texture make vigorous combinations. Lavender stock enlivened with two stems of the red-violet variety have been used with stripped sections of red cabbage, the curled edges and heavy vein system forming a fine textural pattern in the center of the arrangement. Heads of pale-blue hydrangea rest at the base and against the edge of the container of cryptomeria wood, which has been polished and waxed to lustrous richness.

STRELITZIA

The Hindus include fruit in their votive offerings to their deities. Fruit, then, occupies a conspicuous position in this design set in a tall bronze temple-vase from India. The only plant material is the startling bird of paradise. The birds have been pulled out from the sheaths. Poised for flight or turning inquisitively to the fruit, they furnish brilliant color. Limes, lemons, and tangerines, together with red grapes, provide the substance of the temple gift.

Strelitzia

THE STRELITZIA needs an environment of quiet refinement. It should not be alone; it craves suitable neighbors, for it looks its best in an atmosphere of taste and distinction. That type of planting requires space, large landscape effects to provide striking background for this unusual flower. The strelitzia belongs to the banana family, but it is much neater, more trim than the banana. It grows successfully in limited areas of the United States. Where it has to spend most of its time in the warm greenhouse, it can be moved outdoors for the summer and used as a specimen plant. Since it wants full sun all the year, it thrives only in frost-free areas. Plant it in strong, rich soil and give it large amounts of water all summer.

Though several varieties of strelitzia are found in its native South Africa, only one, the bird of paradise, is seen with any frequency in the United States. The leaves, often twelve inches, top long stalks much taller than the leaves. The flower is elaborate. Heading the stalk is a large sheathing bract shaped much like a boat, six inches long and nearly horizontal on the stem. It is showy in color, purple at the base. As it opens, the real blossoms emerge, several from the one spathe. The corolla has three petals: two are usually a vivid blue, tongue-shaped; the third, standing erect above the others, is either white or yellow. The leaves are stiff; the flower stands rigid and waxen. With its pattern of sharp triangles it holds a shapely beauty of aloof elegance appropriate to the daring simplicity of the contemporary home.

The strelitzia lasts well if carefully manipulated. With his fingers the arranger must force out by gentle pressure the flowers encased within the boat. As each blossom fades, remove it and force out the next one.

Strelitzia

Strelitzia and Tropical Fruit

Succulents

In a country as large as the United States the areas of limited rain develop an extensive life adapted to dryness. Plants survive either by so modifying their structure that they require almost no water, or by storing moisture within their stems. In either state an amazing mechanical ingenuity is evidenced in these accommodative processes. We notice, for example, that many desert growths have very shiny surfaces, almost as if varnished; while others have dispensed with leaf structure. They develop very slowly, but they keep alive, just as do the cacti and all the other thick-stemmed succulents with their fleshy reservoirs.

Some of the plants have curious shapes, interesting for their strangeness, like the desert pelargonium with stems like organ pipes; or bodies distorted to grotesque planes and angles that amaze the unbelieving observer who sees them for the first time. Others are attractive enough to excite genuine admiration. The aloe makes a patterned rosette, the pointed segments sometimes precisely overlapping in close scallops; in other kinds the tips are separated and spread in a rather unorganized but picturesque disposal. Perhaps the most widely known of these succulents is the houseleek called familiarly hen-and-chickens; it has an impressive array of cousins used for rock gardens and cover growth, sometimes for edging. The sedums are more diverse in form than the aloes or the houseleeks. The trailing kinds are apt mediums for baskets or living permanent arrangements in vases; the low ones edge; and some of the tallest are suitable for border planting.

The flowering habits of succulents are as diverse as their shapes. Many of the common garden types have small, sometimes inconspicuous, but often delicately attractive flowers; some develop astonishingly beautiful displays of large blossoms in brilliant colors. The small succulents are good house-residents, companionable when several tiny specimens jostle snugly in one planter. They are desirable principally for their foliage, which is interesting and always in good condition.

SUCCULENTS

Polished whorls of a large shell establish the principal lines of the pattern. The shell serves further to conceal the holder. Five blades of aloe, over-lapping, parallel the curve of the shell. Their colors are rich, some red-brown, others green, but all edged with sharp cutting-points of red-brown barbs. Heaped rosettes of æonium fill the space around the shell and complete the swirling circles of the composition.

Succulents

Succulents and Sansevieria

Sunflower

THE MAIDEN Clytie so deeply worshipped Apollo, the sun god, that she spent the entire day facing his bright presence. In pity for her hopeless infatuation, so runs the ancient myth, the god changed her to a flower with a face like his own radiance. At any rate the botanical name of the plant, helianthus, means sunflower. Today sunflowers are grown for commerce and for beauty. Despite the predilection for sunflowers in Russia, India, and Egypt, where the seeds are marketed to be eaten like nuts or crushed for their oil, the United States has little economic interest in the plant. American liking is merely floricultural. Americans experience a naïve delight in the showy giant, especially the tall specimens whose fat, roguish faces can literally sway the plant to destruction. Cultivation is simple. Scatter the seeds in a rich, moist soil, deeply dug, and stake the young stalks solidly. They uproot in wind; they are pulled out of the ground by the weight of their own flowering heads. The typical sunflower is bright yellow with a disk center of yellow or brown, purple, or almost black; but new hybrids occur in many tones of yellow and in several of the darker shades of red.

Another plant often called sunflower is the rudbeckia. A low variety, one to three feet, is the black-eyed Susan of the dusty roadside. A taller kind, the brown-eyed Susan, reaches five feet. These flowers, so closely resembling the helianthus in most respects, differ in the shape of the central disk—flat in the helianthus; cone-shaped in the rudbeckia.

Mexico has its sunflower, the tithonia, which grows also in Central America and the West Indies. It is a tall plant, shrubby at the base, with brilliant flowers of orange-red and scarlet.

Sunflowers make satisfying designs. Defoliate the stems and immerse in deep water. Then arrange either very simply, like daisies, or more vividly to exhibit some stunning color combination.

Sunflower

Sunflower and Dock

SUNFLOWER

Colorful growth of back yard and fence row makes a sprightly design of gay informality. Sunflowers loosely placed are supported by sprays of dock that extend the base, then fill the area to the central placement by easy transitional lines. The dock repeats the deep-brown heart of the sunflowers. The color scheme is softened first by small heads of yarrow placed between the sunflowers and the dock, then by the straw-colored beards of dried barley outlining the lines of principal interest. A copper fish-baker, brilliantly polished, is used as container.

Sweet Pea

THE SWEET pea has few rivals in popularity among the annuals. Whether home-grown or commercially produced, it affords general delight. Known and cultivated for well over two hundred years, it persisted as a small, smooth-petaled flower of limited color range. The extraordinary improvement of the blossom belongs to the twentieth century, with the introduction of the Spencers. The sweet pea demands cool weather. Only in belts of low temperature does it succeed during the summer months. Its general cultural desires are more precise than are the needs of many annuals. It requires a deep, rich soil conditioned with plant food and well watered, for the sweet pea is a heavy feeder. Also, plant early. Only by these means can large, long-stemmed blossoms be expected. While it is not an easy plant for the beginning gardener, a long row of vivid color gives unalloyed satisfaction even to the expert.

The sweet pea is a ready medium for plant design. The color range is unusually varied. White and cream; delicate pastels in pink, salmon, and lavender; deep reds, scarlets, maroons, purples: all these come in solid colors. Other than the plain blooms are parti-colored tints, striped effects, mottled tones. Or one may choose his flowers for their form—the plain-petaled, the wavy-petaled, the ruffled. Like all climbing or trailing plants, the sweet pea lends itself to informal arrangements. In these designs it is best used alone. Large sections of the plant, complete with leaves, flowers, and tendrils, slip naturally into tall, slender containers. A safe guide to follow in combining sweet peas with other materials is to preserve the generous spacing of the upper plant growth where the foliage is scanty and the flowers seem to tiptoe upon their stems. Small leaves of other plants, then, rather than flowers may be used, often with charming effect when set in ground-cover fashion at the base of the arrangement.

Sweet Pea

Sweet Pea and Geranium Leaves

SWEET PEA

A gift basket of extreme delicacy is fashioned of simple flowers in soft tints. Pink and orchid sweet peas in generous massing fill the basket; a few long-stemmed blossoms reach out to the upper placement, where they show among the roses and the pale scabiosas. Fine sprays of syringa complete the vertical portion of the design. In much the same way cuttings of plumbago spill over the rim of the crescent to add one more color to the almost complete range of tints in the design.

TUBEROSE

A highly stylized arrangement uses tuberoses and leaves of the variegated aspidistra. The aspidistra is placed first in the container, a bronze urn, with the leaves so precisely set that the light strips match. Then the tuberoses in shapely branches stand against the dark half of the wide leaves. A folded leaf makes an effective link between the vertical placement and the material swung loosely down the side of the container.

Tuberose

IN THE normal course of events the United States imports tulips from Holland, lilies from China, lily of the valley from Germany, other various and sundry plants from outside our borders; but the tuberose is on the export list. It is kinfolk to the amaryllis, a tender tuber, native of Mexico and growing only in warm sections. Like most other members of its family the tuberose bears its principal foliage in a broad basal rosette. The leaves, twelve to eighteen inches long and a half inch wide, look like speared tufts of grass, bright green with blades reddened at the base. From each rosette rises a single stalk three to four feet high, with blossoms clustering closely in a short terminal raceme. The flowers are white, delicately waxen in texture, and shining in the light. Their small funnels crowding each other on the stem are almost overpoweringly fragrant. The few leaves that may grow on the flower stalk are smaller than the basal foliage and cling closer to the stem. Variegated foliage occurs in a few kinds.

The tuberose appears only infrequently in home gardens. Because it needs much warmth during the growing period, it usually is set out in June; thus it comes into flower in late summer or early autumn. Before the first frost the tuber must be lifted for winter storage in a warm but dry location. Because of the difficulty of wintering the tubers, it is more provident to buy new stock each year than to carry over the old lot. The tuberose is obtainable always in the market and at seasons greatly extended, both early and late, beyond the possibility of home production.

The tuberose raceme is small, but the flower is refined and delicately elegant. It should be arranged with a fastidious attention to detail in a container simple in form and reserved in color but unmistakably patrician in general tone.

Tuberose

Tuberose and Dill

Tulip

THE TULIP was a beautiful gift to early civilization. Where it originated, no man can say. In wild state it grew through Asia from the Mediterranean to Siberia and Japan, but when Europeans first became aware of the flower it was a lovely plaything of the Turks. The Turks must have been cultivating it for a long time. They had developed a definite shape, petals with slender, narrowly pointed tips, and two colors, red and yellow. In the middle of the sixteenth century the Austrian ambassador, returning from Constantinople to Vienna, brought a few tulip seeds with him that he said he had obtained at great price. Europe straightway set to work to modify the Turkish flower. The immediate purpose of Western development was to change both form and color. The rounded petals developed by the Dutch growers are still favorite; the colors were extended until the range, except for blue, was complete. As yet, no blue tulips have been marketed, though there are numerous tones of lavender and purple. Whatever the color, the flowers are brilliant, the most showy of the spring blossoms. Through a careful selection of early and late varieties, the gardener can have six weeks or so of lively bloom.

Like many other bulbs the tulip needs cold weather. In warm belts the flowers are likely to open before the stem has time to rise to full height. Leaves and flowers are produced on the same stalk; and if the bud has not pushed high enough above the top leaf to afford attractive stem length, the leaves will be cut with the flowers. Use of many complete stalks will prevent recuperation of the bulb for the following year.

To condition, immerse the stems deeply. Arrange in shallow water in a pattern of simple dignity, for the tulip is formal in its beauty, from the clean lines of its cup to the symmetry of each petal and the precise contour of the corolla.

TULIP

The rich-toned Japanese plum has supplied the foliage for this arrangement of springtime growth. The fineness of the leaves, their thinness, require a massing of leafage to establish a line of sufficient importance for the tulips, which in brilliant color repeat the line pattern of the plum. To fill the area at the base are two exquisite clusters of clivia. For the small transitional points between tulips and clivia, tulip blossoms have been opened to make a flat, rounded detail.

Tulip. Tulip with Daffodils and Iris

Vegetables

ANYONE who understands the principles of design can make hand-some, sometimes highly dramatic, arrangements of vegetables. The floral artist does not work here to set a lovely flower against a background of foliage, nor to group pretty blossoms that seem to belong together. He must think only in terms of line, mass, color, and texture.

If he needs a rounded green object, should it be a bell pepper, an artichoke, an avocado, a small head of broccoli, or some Brussels sprouts? Think first of the skin alone. Does he want an arrangement composed entirely of glossy objects rubbed until they gleam under the lights? Then he will combine such vegetables as eggplant and peppers. Or does he need only a single detail of mirrorlike quality?

One who works with vegetables will find the squash family his great-est ally for all seasons of the year. Warm days supply the zucchini; the beautifully scalloped summer squash, creamy, slightly greenish of skin; and the yellow crookneck squash, toned from pale yellow to deep orange, with tiny puckers and furrows. Autumn and winter bring the golden pumpkins; the small acorn-squash, deeply cleft into sharp ridges, its colors shaded from dull green to deep orange according to its maturity; then the heavy-skinned squashes covered with nubbles.

Blue is often a problem in vegetable design, for apart from eggplant and purple cabbage, there is little choice. Turnips have a small patch of blue at the stem end; some of the dark-red onions tend toward purple, at least sufficiently for a harmonizing combination; and beets, the very rich ones, do not quarrel. But tomatoes, radishes, and most varieties of rhubarb contain too much yellow, or—as strawberry rhubarb—are too pink to join the blue-purple group.

After the color scheme has been decided, then work as with floral material for an attractive disposition of forms.

Vegetables

VEGETABLES

The attractiveness of this design lies in its complete smartness. A wooden dough-bowl serves as container for its hard practicality. Four kinds of squash are the most noticeable details, each conspicuous for a different reason: the crookneck and the zucchini because of contrasting colors; the acorn from its principal position; the round, summer squash through isolation. Lettuce and a pepper fill the nooks. A final flourish is given by the diagonals made by the sansevieria leaves as they streak out of the container.

Water Lily

A GOOD collection of water lilies contains tropical and temperate species chosen for color, growing habits, and cultural requirements. The flowers are showy, from white through pink to red, yellow, blue, and violet. Some kinds float their blossoms on the water; others lift their faces into the air. Both flowers and leaves rise from thick rootstalks well below the surface. Usually the leaves are two-colored, often purple underneath and lustrous green above. Each species has its own well-regulated behavior: some open in daylight; others at night. With almost clocklike precision each flower unfolds several times, varying its opening and closing not more than a few minutes each day. When the blossoming period is over, it slips below the water to produce seeds.

The United States is well supplied with native water lilies. Because of the great spread of climate, the flowering stage is much longer than in other countries, from early April until late fall. Sections of cool nights produce the most beautiful lilies and the longest seasons of bloom. Once established, the plants are easy to maintain, for they have only three cultural requirements: abundant rich soil, water, and full sunlight. They succeed best when set in boxes three feet square and one foot deep, one plant to a box with spaces between the boxes to permit ample spread. If the pond is deep, the boxes should be placed on supports at a proper level below the surface to permit the flower heads to reach the surface easily. Placing the soil in boxes instead of in the pool itself keeps the water clear. With this method of planting, also, the earth can be kept rich enough to satisfy the gross appetites of the water lilies.

Because the flowers and leaves wilt as soon as cut, they should be plunged immediately into deep water to fill the stems. An arrangement to suggest the lily's growing habits is easily effected through a combination with other aquatic material.

Water Lily

Water Lily and Cane Grass

WATER LILY

Slender green rods of the equisetum in close bundles shelter the flowers.
One broken stem typifies the imperfection of all that is lovely. Frail blossoms of morea, their delicate lavender tints a pale glow, stand against the
deep tones of the reeds. A water lily, fully open and protected by its buds
and leaves, points to the tips of the equisetum, which partially conceals the
other lily plant with its furled leaves, its tight bud, and its opening
flower.

YUCCA

Leaves of the blue cabbage enshrine the bells of the yucca. Bent to the table in secure base, overlapped in rising tiers to disclose the successive placements of the yucca, the crinkled cabbage pleases with its patterned vein tissue. Rising also from the table first in single scattered flowers, then in masses of fully open blossoms, the yucca lifts its lovely spire: fine branches of buds almost tenuous in their delicacy; flowers of incredible purity.

Yucca

Yucca and Leaves

Yucca

HE YUCCA belongs to the stretches of arid desert and the great plains of North America. On the Mexican tablelands, in the West Indies, through the southern and south-central parts of the United States, grow these unique plants, some known for the exquisite delicacy of their flowers, others for their weirdly shaped bodies. Most of the family have a basal structure of foliage; the leaves emerge stemless from the ground—hard, tough, and leathery swords, rough-edged for handling. Their gray-green color suggests the earth to which they are closely related. From the center of this clump rises a flowering stalk covered with delicately cupped blossoms.

The Spanish bayonet, frequently seen in gardens and parks of the southwest, is one of the few yuccas to form a trunk. The leaves are margined yellow or white and tipped with a very sharp point. The flower cluster is showy with white or violet-tinted florets. In the extreme southwest is the great yucca, one of the most precious gifts the earth can offer to mankind. The tall stalk towering over the sand and the dust is a spire of waxen cups delicate beyond anything seen in the ordinary garden. It is called "Our Lord's Candlestick." In these same gray wastes is another yucca, the Joshua tree. Weirdly contorted, its branches strained into grotesque posturings, this Caliban of the desert lures its devotees with the magic of its fairy cups.

To prepare the yucca flowers for arrangements, open the blossoms with the fingers until the inner heart is revealed. Within the pure cup is a slender pistil of the same clear lime green as the veining on the back of the petals. Like gardenias, these flowers last without water. Single blooms alone or in combination make beautiful flat designs in low bowls. Bold effects are easily accomplished, for the same architectural qualities that suit the yucca to formal garden effects make it impressive within the house in massive ornamentation.

Zinnia

OST of our common garden flowers are hundreds of years old with a racial heredity that covers half the world. It is, then, unusual to find a flower that is very popular, yet comparatively recent in origin and restricted in growth. Such a flower is the zinnia. It belongs chiefly to Mexico, though some kinds are native to Chile. The first varieties appeared around 1860, but the large garden zinnia was not introduced until 1886.

Zinnias will grow almost anywhere, in rich soil or sandy. They love sun, not objecting much even to pronounced heat, if they are liberally irrigated in hot, dry weather. Since they do most of their blooming in the warmest time of year, they need care to keep them in full flower. More varied in height than many annuals, they are effective in borders with tall varieties, up to three feet, behind other flowers; or the dwarf zinnias, under eighteen inches, tucked in the front row. If space is no consideration, zinnias can be induced to make sizable plants. The foliage is bright and attractive, cool-looking in the heat of summer. In large gardens of formal design the low-growing zinnias make dramatic color accents when planted in beds of single hue. They are showy: white, all tones of yellow, orange, red, lavender, violet, and purple. No blue zinnia has been shown. Until recently the pink shades were unsatisfactory, but new hybrids in pastel tints are a decided improvement over the older varieties. Flowers of solid color are preferable to the variegated forms.

As a cut flower the zinnia is difficult to manipulate. It wilts rapidly; burning the stem is no protection. The best preventive is complete immersion of the branch after the leaves have been removed. Because of the stiffness and rigidity of the stalks, the zinnia is best suited to designs of simple line.

ZINNIA

Late summer arrangements can display all the richness of autumn coloring. A quaint brown basket holds the container for these flowers. Primary placements, in loosely assembled diagonal lines, are made with zinnias red-orange and yellow in tone. An even more brilliant central detail contains yellow plume celosia and orange cannas. The fiery sheen of the canna blossoms is almost dazzling in full illumination; velvet tips of celosia fitted around this gorgeous center build a soft transition to the darker laterals.

Zinnia

Zinnia and Barley

The Arrangements in the Photographs

*A description in detail of each of the black-and-white illustrations
that accompanies the text and color plates.*

ACANTHUS (*Acanthus mollis*)

Acanthus blossoms with their leaves are simply arranged in a clear glass brick to emphasize the individual forms of each. Submerging of the lower leaf serves to conceal the pinpoint holder and gives etched relief to an otherwise commonplace container.

ACANTHUS AND *Melianthus major*

In this arrangement the accent on blossoms alone is reminiscent of the classic pattern of this traditionally sculptured flower. The line flows rhythmically into the circle of the modern container. The blue-green of the pinnated leaf of the honey plant functions as a co-ordinating unit between flowers and container in color, texture, and form.

AGAPANTHUS (*Agapanthus africanus*)

The blue lily of the Nile arranged in a steel-blue pewter container gives a feeling of remote coolness to a refined portrayal of this flower and its own foliage. The flowing pattern is that of restrained linear design.

AGAPANTHUS AND ARALIA LEAVES

A profusion of blossoms and aralia foliage is clustered in a yellow-green pottery container. The irregular distribution of the leafage gives dramatic outline to flowers whose umbellate blooms appear cluttered if used alone in mass. By this treatment distinction is achieved.

AGAVE (*Agave americana*)

The peeled ivory-colored heart of the century plant makes for spectacular display. Each tubular segment of its growth gives structural quality. The tall pinnacles rising from the wooden base convey the impression of architectural forms.

AGAVE AND GLADIOLUS

By removing the tips of the segments of the century plant the designer has achieved a columnar effect. In this arrangement, as in the preceding plate, the effect is architectural. Here the dominant lines are softened by the inclusion of spikes of the salmon-beige gladiolus in a sand-colored container of striated design.

AMARYLLIS

The exotic quality of the amaryllis is expressed by this restrained arrangement of a single stalk. The fully open basal flower was removed from the stem and placed low, where the inversion of the foliage accents the beauty of the blossom. For contrast the red flowers are placed in a green container.

AMARYLLIS AND NEW ZEALAND FLAX (*Phormium tenax*)

Striped blossoms of the hybrid amaryllis find repetition in the striped foliage of the New Zealand flax. This material is arranged in a daring manner, with the weight of the clustered blossoms centered in the pattern to give stability to a design of rapid motion. The blades of the flax have been creased to ensure this unusual effect.

ANTHURIUM (*Anthurium andraea-num*) AND STRELITZIA LEAVES

The almost artificial appearance of these flowers affords a spectacular contribution to the floral world. Four spathes, vibrantly red, are subdued by the heavier background of the folded gray-green leaves of the bird of paradise plant. Veined indentation of the leaf supplements that of the blossom. The pottery container is the color of the foliage.

ANTHURIUM AND YUCCA (*Yucca aloifolia*)

Coral anthurium has been flanked by the ivory-colored, inverted stem ends of the yucca to provide contrast in form and color. The startling effect caused by the lacquered quality of both gives a pleasant impression of unreality. The serrated edges of three slashed green stalks afford contrast to the regular periphery of the other material.

APPLE BLOSSOM (*Malus pumila*)

Tender new growth of apple blossoms springing from a gnarled stump is the subject of this portrayal. Low and in the foreground short clusters of flowering stems are massed. Leaning out, they conceal the water-filled container which, if too obvious, might disturb this poetic treatment of the resurgence of life.

APPLE BLOSSOM AND AZALEA

One branch of apple blossoms is placed erect, yet slightly curved to bring into silhouette other lateral stems projecting from the same stalk. Slightly lower, a few sprays of blush-pink azaleas come to rest at the edge of the water. The crystal container gives weight; its luminosity adds a spiritual quality to the design.

ARTICHOKE (*Cynara scolymus*)

Rough and heavy forms of the artichoke are arranged in a basket of thick, woven strips of cane. The fibrous texture of both the container and the plant material harmoniously combine. The shape of the basket is repeated by the cupped forms of the arranged material.

ARTICHOKE AND PALM FIBER

In a massive low ceramic bowl of lavender-blue glaze, stalks of the artichoke are standing erect. The unexpected lavender-blue of the blossoms, the blue-green of the stalks and crowns, and the looped ribbon of blue-green palm bark give startling color to this virile vertical design.

ASPIDISTRA (*Aspidistra elatior*) AND ARALIA LEAVES

The furled and twisted leaves of the aspidistra, one of the most pliable of all plant materials, lend themselves to horizontal placements in this design. The yellow-green of the aralia, flanked by the dark-green leaves of the aspidistra, springs upward and out from a similarly colored container. Such an arrangement is almost permanent.

ASPIDISTRA AND KNIPHOFIA BLOSSOMS (*Kniphofia uvaria*)

A severe diagonal line is the basis of this design. The upper aspidistra leaves are curled into tubular form and used in reverse to capture their ribbed beauty. The staggered lower leaves are manipulated so that the sheen of the front side of the leaves is emphasized. Blossoms of the yellow-orange red-hot poker, angularly placed, ascend from a yellow-green container.

ASTER (*Callistephus chinensis*)

Purple asters are arranged in a rectangular container of similar color but lighter tone. Starting with the longest and strongest stem, the designer banded the blossoms into the line on the left. By this method weak-stemmed flowers can be supported. A shorter grouping is on the right. Where the two come together, they are given unity by the use of their own foliage.

ASTER AND GLADIOLUS

In this severe vertical pattern white gladioli with violet throats establish the line. Asters spiral from a harmonizing purple-and-white container. The weight of color finds balance by the dominance of the purple asters and their rounded form.

BAMBOO (*Bambusa*)

Two segments of the large bamboo placed side by side in an earthenware plate establish this design. The excess foliage is deftly removed, leaving a fine tracery of green leaves in patterned silhouette.

BAMBOO AND CHRYSANTHEMUMS

Small bamboo is pruned into the classic heaven-man-and-earth pattern, a symbolism repeated in the placement of the three lime-green chrysanthemums. The cane-colored container repeats the color of the bamboo stalk. Bamboo foliage clustered in neat bundles conceals the pinpoint holder.

BANANA (*Musa abyssinica*)

The foliage, fruit, and blossom of the exotic banana plant are arranged in a bold, tropical pattern. The circular line in the folded leaves repeats the growth pattern of the young fruit, a line reflected by the container.

BANANA AND DIEFFENBACHIA LEAVES (*Dieffenbachia picta*)

Segments of the peeled layers of the banana stalk rise like cylinders from a flowing diagonal arrangement of dried pandanus strips formed into curls. Other segments of this same material spiral up to entwine the stalks. These diagonal and vertical lines are united by an abstract form created with Dieffenbachia foliage.

BELLS OF IRELAND (*Molucella lævis*)

A display of the bells of Ireland is a delight to the eye in both color and form. In this twisted arrangement the plant material rises from a container whose line repeats the contour of the bracts. The subtle variation of color found in a single stalk makes the bells invaluable to the arranger.

BELLS OF IRELAND AND POMEGRANATE (*Punica granatum*)

Bells of Ireland function as the dominant placement in an arrangement with pleasing color interest. A brown-stemmed branch of the vivid orange-red pomegranate is defoliated to give color accent. Deep-green hydrangea leaves are placed to either side of the bells of Ireland to intensify the greens. The brown, green-lined container is a perfect foil for this design.

BIRD'S-NEST FERN (*Asplenium nidus*)

The distinguishing beauty of this fern is its molded form. Sculpture-like, it is strongest when arranged to represent its own cycle of development. The beauty of each leaf seems molten; the leaves enfold each other as would cooling metal, and the rippled edges give dimensional value.

Bird's-Nest Fern with Day Lilies (*Hemerocallis flava*)

An exhilarating design employs the bird's-nest fern with day lilies. The unusual angle of the arrangement is a refreshing departure in linear placement. When executed in bold foliage or strong flowers, the effect is highly dramatic.

Bougainvillea

Defoliating the sprays of bougainvillea discloses the tissue texture of each floral bract and simplifies the appearance of the branch. Here a highly patterned vase demanded a conservatism in plant materials. The orange-colored vine finds color detail repeated in this setting.

Bougainvillea and Day Lilies (*Hemerocallis flava*)

The plan for this composition is the placing of the spray material to simulate the recurrent circular lines of the ceramic figure. Just as the orange bougainvillea and day lilies complement the copper plumage of the rooster, so the blue-green bowl and the body of the fowl are of identical glaze.

Broom (*Cytisus scoparius*)

Broom foliage has been bent, fingerlike, into an interesting silhouette. Erect and centered in the green container are bundles of broom foliage cut in staggered lengths surmounted by tall spikes of its fragrant flowers erect in their fragile beauty. Low and at the base these same blossoms repeat the lovely yellow color.

Broom and Pansies (*Viola tricolor hortensis*)

In a yellow vertical container blossoms of broom repeat the erect form of the vase. Yellow and purple pansies, rounded and velvety, are placed where the fluid lines of the broom converge.

Cactus

The cactus is one of the most fascinating materials that bountiful nature provides. An ingenious floral arranger soon learns to select arms or segments of this plant which suggest interesting possibilities. Cactus and palm combine to give an abstract, sculptured form in this simple yet clear-cut design. Water should not be used in this arrangement, as it will hasten deterioration of the fibrous stems of the desert plant.

Cactus and Sea Forms

Because of its weird appearance and varied form, the cactus lends itself to startling composition; the only preparation required of the artist is studied observation. In this realistic design the fan coral is placed diagonally in the background and the foreground, with the fish form of the cactus in opposition to the other major line. Yellow and lime-green cactus blossoms suggest anemone of the sea in this marine display.

Caladium

These leaves are so exquisitely veined and colored that they appear to be painted on the sheerest of fine rice-paper. The container is hand-tinted rose porcelain with an ormolu base and chalice top. The two upper leaves give balance to the base. The placement of the three curved leaves repeats the soft oval line of the container.

CALADIUM WITH CURCULIGO CAPITULATA

Three accordion-bladed leaves of the Australian weevil plant repeat the vertical line of the Chinese figure. Caladium leaves tinged rose-pink, white, and green with their soft coloring contribute to the quiet mood and the serenely Oriental tone of the composition.

CALLA (*Zantedeschia æthiopica*)

Great dignity is effected in this arrangement of calla blossoms and leaves, largely by means of the depth of the pattern. This design is truly dimensional in that the veined leaf is far back; middle distant are the erect placements, and far forward the spiraled blooms. The rounded container is repeated by the whorl in the design.

CALLA AND ASPIDISTRA (*Aspidistra lurida* var. *variegata*)

Calla lilies and variegated aspidistra leaves are shown in a softened diagonal line. The flat, white glaze of the container in its textural value is quite similar to the fine surface of the ivory spathes of the flowers. Furled leaves surround the clustered blooms.

CAMELLIA

Camellia branches and one blossom have been given casual arrangement. Because of the Oriental ancestry of this shrub a three-level pattern has been employed for the foliage placement, with one specimen flower shown

in full beauty. The glass container is compatible with the handsome dark-green foliage.

CAMELLIA AND HEATHER (*Erica*)

One pink camellia centered in the container is given prominence by the delicate placements of the white bouvardia sprays and blooms. The pattern of heather above and below exaggerates the rounded forms of the centered material. A blossom of the camellia rests casually off center, braced against the base of the container.

CANNA

Because of its bold form canna foliage lends itself to striking designs. These bronze-green leaves stand erect in a heavy pottery container that looks like a primitive slab. The taller leaves are in a reverse placement the better to feature their repetitious vertical ribbing and further dramatize the design. Yellow-orange spikes of the canna flower and elongated tight bud-spikes give glowing color.

As with all canna foliage, this green-leafed variety has been completely immersed until firm and then arranged in this triangular pattern, which will last several weeks. Unopened floral spikes are placed beyond the leaf pattern to give depth to the composition. In the foreground fiery red blossoms of this flower are clustered in a celadon container.

CARNATION (*Dianthus caryophyllus*)

Blooms, buds, and foliage of the carnation are set in an antique lamp base that makes an unusual but altogether harmonious container for this old-fashioned and well-known flower. The verticality of the topmost blossoms repeats the erectness of the vase. The lower flowers harmonize with the central contour of the container.

CARNATION AND PITTOSPORUM (*Pittosporum tenuifolium*)

Carnation blossoms flow upward in staggered placements to give a crisp and precisely sweeping effect to this pungent and spicy flower. Green and white sprays of the variegated pittosporum give patterned relief and add stability to the design.

CASTOR BEAN (*Ricinus communis*)

In a fluted Chinese copper container the rich leaves of the castor bean have been set in a soft circular line of bronze, brown, and green tones. The tall upper leaf is placed in silhouette to give the eye a downward sweep into the burred spikes of the seed pods.

The figure of a Balinese girl seems appropriately at home in her dancing position amidst the lush, fingered leaves of castor bean foliage. One curved spike of the red-brown seed pods enriches the golden color and flaring gilt headdress of the dancer. The figurine and the container are identical in color and glaze.

CELOSIA: COCKSCOMB (*Celosia cristata*)

Red cockscomb is arranged in a dignified line in order to show to advantage the crested form of the blossoming spikes. The container is Etruscan, a reproduction from the Metropolitan Museum of Art.

CELOSIA AND LARKSPUR (*Delphinium ajacis*)

A rough-textured pink-beige container supports vertical spikes of pink larkspur. At the lip of the container heavier masses of the celosia ascend, gradually diminishing in width until they seem to flow into the stalks of the flowered larkspur.

CELOSIA: PLUME (*Celosia argentea*) AND PAMPAS (*Cortaderia selloana*)

In a brass container with ram's-head footing the yellow plumed celosia is given a conical form. The plumes of the pampas grass run congruent to the design and give textural delicacy and a champagne tint to this monochromatic study.

CELOSIA AND CHRYSANTHEMUMS

In a four-sided wooden box of planter type with metal liner celosia stems have been impaled to flare out triangularly and give the impression of an abstract tree. Sunk deep within the golden plumes is another severe triangular placement of the gold and rust-red variegated chrysanthemums.

CHARD (*Beta vulgaris* var. *cruenta*)

Green chard made crisp by complete immersion stands erect, with two leaves extending horizontally along the rim of a shallow container. An intricate pattern of bold venation is brought into sharp relief by these placements. Blanched wooden pinnacles, twinlike, of the water cypress give form, weight, and dimension to this virile design.

CHARD (*Beta vulgaris cicla*) AND DAHLIAS

Chard leaves furnish strong background material for large red dahlias. An interesting tactile contrast of foliages is secured by the addition of the shiny leaves of the rubber tree. A fluted pottery receptacle repeats the green of the foliage.

CHRYSANTHEMUM: BALL

Large and showy chrysanthemums, ball type, are centered in the container in a severe vertical line where each flower is spaced to give full value to its beauty of form. Placement of all the stems to spring from a common base accents the cleanliness of the design.

CHRYSANTHEMUM AND CATTAILS
(*Typha latifolia*)

Concealed deep in a rustic bark shell is the more practical container for water. The pyramid of cattails, the rust to yellow chrysanthemums, and the opalescent green grapes all share in common the late autumnal season.

CHRYSANTHEMUM: QUILL

The quill chrysanthemums, richly tawny, are placed in a flat, oblong bowl of similar hue. The pattern of the design is a loose and free variant of the Japanese realistic approach in flower arranging. Leaves conceal each of the two holders used for the flower placements.

CHRYSANTHEMUM AND PAMPAS
(*Cortaderia selloana*)

In a pleasing relationship this flower of Oriental ancestry is placed in a dusty-copper container of Chinese design. The champagne-colored chrysanthemums disclose a neat pattern employing flowers and buds in graduated size. The taffy pampas-plumes give an airiness to this tree design.

CORAL TREE (*Erythrina crista-galli*)

Three sprays of the flamboyant coral tree have been cut in gradient lengths and placed to shorten gradually toward the front. Each spray is bud-tipped; the open blossoms and green leaves are used naturally. Individual clusters of coral tree foliage are massed at the base.

CORAL TREE AND ASPIDISTRA LEAVES
(*Aspidistra elatior*)

A repetitious arcing of aspidistra leaves establishes a dominant note in this design. Sprays of the coral tree outline the leaf pattern and give a fringed effect of vibrant color. Aralia leaves placed back to back hold each other erect in an octagonal container.

CRAPE MYRTLE (*Lagerstrœmia indica*)

Sprays of crape myrtle are placed far to one side of a pressed gray brick container. Since all stems emanate from one central placement and the foliage has been removed for some distance, an austere barrenness has been created that is necessary for good co-ordination between container and the fluffier leafed floral branches.

CRAPE MYRTLE AND PALM (*Chamœdorea elegans*)

Two sprays of the Chamœdorea palm have been trimmed into an oblate shape. These are placed, crescent-like, at the rear of the flower holder. Crape myrtle blossoms are heavily massed in lines congruent to the background material.

CRINUM (*Crinum longifolium*)

An interesting arrangement of crinum shows development through varied bud levels finally climaxed by the umbel of fully opened blossoms. A rounded rock gives austere contrast and lends strength to this unusual composition.

CRINUM AND CABBAGE (*Brassica oleracea capitata*)

Contrasting plant materials achieve perfect balance by massed weights vying one against the other. Three leaves of gray-black cabbage, two rolled into fluted forms, appear on the right. One is cupped forward and in protective fashion shelters the floral heads of the crinum.

CYCLAMEN (*Cyclamen indicum*)

A pink pearl-lined shell becomes a floral container for pink cyclamen blossoms and stalks denoting various stages of growth. Wherever the eye rests, whether it be on curved bud or floral stem or disklike fully opened flower, rhythm and repetition of form are beautifully expressed.

CYCLAMEN WITH TREE BRANCH

An almost white weather-worn branch of a lifeless tree is placed erect at the far left of the container. Its eerie quality is given contrast by the grouping of the cyclamens after their manner of true growth.

CYMBIDIUM (*Cymbidium lowianum*)

The vertical placement of cymbidium orchids consists of one floral spray with many yellow-brown blooms. Massed very low and in the center of the tan and yellow-green striped container are individual blossoms, each separately held by its own stem. Leaf blades of the plant's own foliage flow out one side of the floral arrangement.

CYMBIDIUM AND BIRD'S-NEST FERN (*Asplenium nidus*)

Molded leaf forms of the bird's-nest fern show an outline of three levels with variations in the surfaces of the leaves. The foliage springs cuplike from a narrowed base to a flaring rim of broader and taller leaves. The cymbidium orchids, like pale jewels, are held discreetly low against this carved green frame.

CYPRIPEDIUM (*Cypripedium candidum*)

With yellow-green pouch or slipper, dark-green striping, and white crest this orchid, the cypripedium, is possibly the most refreshing of all the orchid types. Arranged in a crackled glass rectangular container, the plant materials are held in position by a small wooden branch cut the width of the container and securely wedged at water level against the vertical stems.

CYPRIPEDIUM WITH TREE BARK

A thin slab of rustic bark gives a sylvan feeling comparable to the environmental habitat of the cypripedium. This flower when growing wild seeks protective shelter through an affinity with its surroundings. This way of life is suggested by the placement of the flowers against the mottled background. Tufts of moss, while concealing the container, give weight and finish to the design.

DAFFODIL (*Narcissus*)

Daffodils and foliage are grouped with a feeling for natural growth. Where flowers are arranged in this manner, the final effect is more pleasing if they conform to requirements of conventional design. Too casual or haphazard placements would be disturbing.

DAFFODIL AND PALM (*Chamædorea elegans*)

The fronds of clipped Chamædorea palm, rubber leaves, and daffodils are employed in a radiating line. This is an excellent example of the use of foliage for structural pattern. In itself it lasts for weeks. When scarcity of bloom is a consideration, a few flowers may be added from time to time as in the case of the daffodil placements.

Dahlia

Large, striated dahlias are arranged at varied angles to show individual beauty of bloom. Buds and flowers in varying stages of development give grace, depth, and contour to the floral plan. Dahlia foliage is used low and at the base.

Both small and large dahlias combine effectively in this design. Transition in form is accomplished by the opening bud at the terminal end of the large dahlia placements. It coordinates the sharper, disklike forms and the larger, softer quills of the more basal flowers.

Daisy (*Chrysanthemum*)

Delicate pale-yellow daisies radiate from a reed basket of similar color and harmonious texture. A centered larger flower of the same family gives weight and unifies the whole. Small groups of flowers with varied stem lengths have been assembled in spikes before their insertion into the container.

Daisy with Tree Branch

A branch of an apple tree selected in early summer shows a small formation of fruits and sprays of lingering bloom. Low and at the base the little daisies are grouped and so arranged that they appear to be growing from out the ground.

Datura (*Datura arborea*)

Angel's trumpets silently spell their ethereal name in this arrangement. In circular pattern one long spray leans out pendent as they grow, with the flowers facing toward the earth. Other blooms massed as an angelic choir point skyward and seem to voice the radiance of eternity.

Datura and Aspidistra (*Aspidistra lurida* var. *variegata*)

Three leaves of the variegated green-and-white aspidistra flow upward with great strength and dimensional form. Softly furled green-ribbed buds and white, fully opened blooms of the datura suggest the quality of purity so apparent in the living blossoms.

Delphinium

Delphinium in tints of white to light blue together with its own foliage spirals up from a unique container of white porcelain. A study of this design will give the arranger the knowledge of dimension and form so necessary in achieving good pattern regardless of the type of plant material employed.

Delphinium and Daisies (*Chrysanthemum*)

This design shows a delightful combination of plant materials and container. The sharp diagonal line gives strong motion and gaiety to these summertime flowers of delphinium and daisy. Wisps of honey-colored barley give airiness and harmony to both flowers and container.

Dried Arrangements: Temperate

The long sprays of tawny sea oats face one another in the dominant background placement. Recessed into the oats are several sprays of the bells of Ireland. Dark-brown leaves of rolled and furled aspidistra enrich the material and unify it with its wooden container into a design of permanent beauty.

Ever shedding bark from the eucalyptus tree gives many interesting tubular forms. Its exterior color is gray-white; its inner recessions a rich brown. One dried conical form of an almost white yucca spike is vertically erect with its base surrounded by small splinters of bark. The container is a low disk of rough-textured sandlike material.

Dried Arrangements: Tropical

Two leaf-protecting sheaths of a tropical ornamental palm are the background feature, their recessed color a rich cocoa brown intensified by dried and massed clusters of dombeya blooms. At the base two honey-colored dombeya leaves indicate the bamboo vase of identical hue.

Affecting the strong velocity of rising winds, two sprays of dried palm flower-bearing clusters describe a sweeping curve. Loops of dark-brown, dried banana sheaths continue this line and give harmony of color to the spathe of the royal palm. A coconut blown from its tree rests where it fell; as if by accident it contributes form and great stability to the design. The flower holder is concealed by dombeya blooms.

Embryo Palm

Reptilian as an Oriental dragon, three embryo palm branches pose sinuously in a crude earthen bowl. Frond segments on the lower right placement suggest the thorny spines cresting the head of this snarling creature of Indonesian myth and folklore.

Embryo Palm with Leaves

Two fronds of embryo palm, weird in form, beckon malevolently to the forces of evil. Plumeria leaves and fruits of the earth symbolize the good and rest firmly secure in this Balinese design depicting the opposing forces of nature.

Eucalyptus (*Eucalyptus ficifolia*)

A hollowed stump of the eucalyptus supplies water for this arrangement, consisting of furled bark, leaves, buds, and blossoms of this Australian tree. The vivid splash of red stamens and deep-green leaves is vibrant against the grayed bark and the container of muted tone.

Eucalyptus with Aucuba Leaves (*Aucuba japonica* var. *punctata*)

Yellow-speckled green leaves of the aucuba arranged in a soft semicircle flow upward in an arc. Centered and surrounded by these leaves rests a vivid cluster of the orange-red eucalyptus flowers and bracts. This design offers an unusual treatment for a pedestaled container.

Francoa

Starry sprays of the white francoa rocket up from their narrow base in a vertical relieved by the downward curve of the lowest branch. The container, a simple rounded line in austere contrast, further emphasizes the floral pattern.

Placements of francoa, lyrelike in background silhouette, give an appropriate setting for the statue of Saint Francis meditatively reading while little doves perch around him. The container is brown and pale pink: the undersurface repeats the tones of the friar's gown; the lining echoes the flesh tones of the head and the pink hearts of the flowers.

Frangipani (*Plumeria acutifolia*)

The horizontal line of this design suggests the somnolence of the tropics. The lushness of the banana stalk used as a container reflects the glint of the tropical sun. Over all hangs the leaden perfume of frangipani blossoms. One vertical cluster enlivens the severity of the prevailing laterals.

Frangipani with Hibiscus

The ruins of a Malayan temple hidden by ever encroaching tropical flora are suggested by this ancient Buddhist mask surrounded by the dark-green frangipani leaves and its heavily scented waxen flowers. Hibiscus blossoms, paperlike, seem nature's ritualistic offering to an altar god.

Fruit

In a green ceramic lacework tray leaves of the aspidistra rolled into furls embellish an arrangement of apples. The two uppermost fruits are impaled on sticks. This is an excellent example of the importance of the proper distribution of masses and space.

This fruit arrangement displays a richness in color value. Bananas, peaches, and lustrous green grapes are climaxed by variegated tan and green cymbidium orchids. When arranging fruits, one follows elements of design just as when arranging flowers.

Geranium (*Pelargonium hortorum*)

Two branches of geranium seem casually placed in a Japanese bowl. Al-though the design seems careless, a trained eye was required to remove diverse lateral growths that, if left, would have resulted in confusion. A rosette of blossoms surrounded by a fringe of leaves gives a restful close-up of this charming flower.

Geranium with Scabiosas (*Scabiosa atropurpurea*)

Scabiosa and winglike forms of ornamental begonia provide the structural background lines for a vertical clustering of geranium blooms. The latter should be plucked in bud stage to ensure the bloom cycle and eliminate petal shattering.

Gerbera (*Gerbera jamesoni*)

Muted coral-pink double Transvaal daisies combine with the grayed leaves of the dusty miller. The latter are so similar to the daisy's own foliage that the finished effect is almost identical with an arrangement entirely of gerbera material. The low bowl discloses gray and coral-pink bands of color.

Gerbera with Aucuba Leaves (*Aucuba japonica* var. *punctata*)

Economy of plant material in utilizing to advantage the unusual curved stems of the gerbera is the value of this design. The reddest of daisies rest in the foreground backed by dappled aucuba leaves.

Ginger: Red (*Zingiber alpinia purpurata*)

In a dark-brown wooden bowl six plumes of ruby-red ginger are placed. On the left the ginger foliage, graduated in size, tapers to a pointed tip; on the right the blooms echo the pattern of the shiny green leaves. A gnarled tree knot provides a basal finish.

GINGER WITH CROTON LEAVES
(*Codiæum variegatum pictum*)

Red ginger springs out from a central placement to give a diagonal pattern. The red-black leaves of the croton execute a similar plan. The burnished copper container, simple in form, strengthens this dramatic design.

GINGER: SHELL (*Zingiber alpinia nutans*)

One of the most interesting of the ginger family is the shell type. Its delicate color, ivory sheen, and beaded pattern give it novel interest. This design shows its folded leaves and tightly encased buds, one opening and one fully out. Low at the base the protective sheath covering each bud has been used for color and tubular effect.

GINGER WITH CROTON LEAVES

In a vertical vase tall spikes of the shell ginger graduated in development repeat the structure of the container. The blossoms droop in cascade fashion out to the right. Highly colored green and yellow croton leaves are set apart, the better to contrast the strange tassels of the flowered material. The blossoms of this ginger are more beautiful in arrangements when artificially removed from their protective sheaths.

GLADIOLUS

A budded spike and attached foliage of the gladiolus was selected for the uppermost placement because of its unusual form. One almost fully blown florescence stands erect. The tip end and tracery of the tallest line extends the direction of the lower terminal bud.

GLADIOLUS AND WATER LILIES
(*Nymphæa*)

Six gladioli, their stems made short, establish the linear plan for this design. The spikes were impaled at varied angles to give individual contour to each floral placement. Water lilies, radiantly beautiful, complete the triangular form.

HELICONIA (*Heliconia bihai humilis*)

The dramatic pattern of background material is achieved by placing the bird of paradise leaves progressively in silhouetted pairs. The exotic form of the heliconia, whose single bracts repeat the shape of the folded leaves, strengthens the design. The two largest leaves support the flower stalks, conceal the holder, and give firmness and brilliant finish.

HELICONIA AND ASPIDISTRA LEAVES
(*Aspidistra elatior*)

This diagonal line achieves a heightened feeling of motion because of the amazingly fishlike forms of the heliconia. Two aspidistra leaves on the upper left find their reflection in the same material folded and impaled with a flourish at the edge of the container.

HIBISCUS

Long needlelike reeds achieved by stripping the foliage from the supporting rib of leaf segments of the coconut palm are used in the Polynesian fashion for impaling hibiscus in elongated and showy placements. One perfect bloom and its dark-green glossy leaves rest low in the clear glass container.

HIBISCUS WITH LEAVES

Long fluted ti leaves assume an erect placement, with flatter leaf-blades of this plant placed horizontally. Yellow and green croton leaves with red-orange venations repeat an inner triangular pattern. Beautiful peach-tinted hibiscus blooms lend their transient forms as floral interest. These are changed daily, for the background material is of long duration.

HOLLY (*Ilex aquifolium*)

Several tall individual and berried sprays of the English holly have been entwined for fullness and columnar effect, then impaled as one placement to establish a firm vertical line that repeats the volume of the rounded form of the pedestal. On the left a few sprays fall out as though unintentionally. The burnished gold container is an appropriate vessel for this glossy and red-berried shrub.

Since water is not a consideration for this seasonal suggestion, a yellow-green leafwork ceramic bowl has been overturned to provide a suitable base for this formal holly tree. Clusters of its own vivid red berries are contrasted by yellow-green ornaments, which, in turn, harmonize container and tree.

HOLLYHOCK (*Althœa rosea*) WITH LEAVES

Among the familiar garden flowers the hollyhock undoubtedly is the most overlooked by those who arrange flowers, perhaps because of the great size of the stalk. Only the delicate floral portion should be used. In this design blue-green loquat leaves with exquisite veining combine with the petal pattern of the old-fashioned blossoms whose basic form and beautiful coloring are as ageless as time. Hollyhock coloring is unusually lovely; these flowers shade from pink to a deeper rose.

The incongruous combination of rough leaf and delicate flower, together with poor lasting quality, might account, in part, for the general dislike of the hollyhock as an acceptable medium for flower arrangements. With defoliation and complete immersion this material becomes a charming subject for floral treatment. Canna leaves, velvet-textured leaves from the tree cineraria, clustered blooms of the hollyhock are included in this horizontal design.

HYDRANGEA (*Hydrangea macrophylla*)

In a reversal of the usual approach to floral art a vase of rare glaze and color is treated more importantly than the arrangement. Its cylindrical form is opposed in the concave surface of the thin sheath of brown bark. The bluest of hydrangea blossoms so perfectly match the blue glaze in the upper section of the container that glossy green hydrangea leaves were needed to define the difference between the two.

HYDRANGEA WITH CROTALARIA (*Crotalaria candicans*)

With deep-blue flecks and the greenest of yellows, the coloring of the floral spikes of the canary bird stalks seem painted. Dark-green hydrangea leaves bring into prominence French hybrid hydrangeas of delft blue in this presentation of color which is as Eastern as a Persian pattern.

Iris

An arrangement of iris as practiced by masters of the Japanese classical schools is the subject of this presentation. One stalk consists of bud and flower stands; a third flower holding its blossom erect faces the overhead sun with each leaf blade a studied placement in natural growth. This seemingly simple arrangement requires a vast background knowledge.

Iris and Equisetum (*Equisetum præaltum*)

Completely unlike the preceding presentation is this free and unrestrained arrangement of Japanese iris blooms and equisetum, both aquatic. In this design the plant material also looks skyward, but with a radiance that is not earthbound. Iris blades and a mound of rocks stabilize this Occidental expression.

Ivy (*Hedera helix*)

The ivy, one of the most satisfactory of all vines for exterior planting, is equally desirable as cut or growing material within the home. Long sprays of this deeply green leathery plant are angularly placed in an iron well-bucket, with a massing of individually stemmed leaves in a rosette placement to give balance to this functional design.

Any vine may be arranged to simulate height by entwining its stem around a tree or any other erect form. A branch of weathered manzanita is placed in a flower holder; then a long spray of ivy is induced to cling to the limbs of the tree. A slab of bark placed horizontally conceals holder and water receptacle in a design that may last indefinitely.

Jacaranda (*Jacaranda acutifolia*)

The blossoming clusters of this tree display a value of blue-violet infrequently seen in floral color. A section of an aged tree stump is placed horizontally. Branches of jacaranda flowers almost barren of foliage during the blooming period protrude from the right. A grouping of the fernlike foliage is placed on the left.

Jacaranda and Lilies

Three floral umbels of this South American tree rest against a barren branch selected for its lines and frontal angle. Orange lilies beneath the tree suggest their habitat and contrast with the blue-violet of the jacaranda flower.

Jacobinia (*Jacobinia carnea*)

The jacobinia is interesting through its entire cycle of growth. The leaves are of great interest, ranging from tan through green to a rich burgundy shade. The basal support for the dusty-rose flowers resembles a leafed cone. In this design the stalks are arranged to show the details of the plant, both leaves and flower cones.

Jacobinia and Chrysanthemums

The dusty-rose floral petals of the jacobinia in its first stage emerge from their nubbly cone like a pattern of fine needlepoint embroidery. As the buds mature, long segments, honeysuckle in form, thrust upward in tubular spikes. The stems and leaves with the dusty-pink chrysanthemums and a pink vase give a complementary harmony.

KNIPHOFIA (*Kniphofia uvaria*)

The distinctive form and radiantly warm coloring of the red-hot poker make it outstanding in its candelabrum arrangement. From crested mane to pointed tip each floral spike enhances this design planned on a rhythm of curves. The placement of four blooms at the bases gives asymmetrical balance.

KNIPHOFIA AND CASTOR BEAN

The placement of two severely trimmed castor bean stalks establishes two levels in this design. One kniphofia spike curved to the right denotes a third level. Although this arrangement follows a triangular form, its line is vertical. The container is a hand-turned ceramic bowl of red-orange.

LARKSPUR (*Delphinium cultorum*)

Sprays of both the pale and the deep-pink larkspur are arranged in stimulating zigzag fashion. The lighter tinted flowers appear high on the left and descend on the right. The deeper-toned spires flow upward from the vase, gradually terminated by a delicate transition in the paler spikes.

LARKSPUR AND CARNATIONS

Rose-pink larkspur and blush-pink carnations are arranged in a candle holder. The tall larkspur placement is set taperlike to harmonize with the holder. Carnations starting low and at the base of the handle curve up congruent to the background line. On the left a spike of larkspur prolongs the curve that starts at the handle and swings through the three basal carnations.

LILAC (*Syringa vulgaris*)

Branches of lilac with their flowered racemes are gracefully grouped in a natural manner. Elimination of some foliage was necessary in order to disclose the full beauty of the floral spikes. Cork bark is fashioned into a log container.

LILAC AND TULIPS (*Tulipa*)

Although the lilac has been completely defoliated in this arrangement, its linear distribution is the same as in the preceding plate. Yellow tulips are assembled after the same plan in this combination of seasonal bloom.

LILY: PLAIN (*Lilium longiflorum eximium*)

The purity of the blossom of the Easter lily is advantageously expressed in this design. A Y-shaped branch inserted near the lip of the container supports the floral stems in a container of Swedish glass with a sanded finish.

LILY AND CANE GRASS (*Arundo donax variegata*)

In this presentation loops of cane, ribbon-fashion, encircle the base of the design. Triangularly massed, the lily blooms ascend to a bud tip in a vertical prolonged by a stalk of variegated green-and-white-striped cane.

LILY: VARIEGATED (*Lilium auratum*)

Sprays and blooms of the dappled and richly fragrant auratum lilies are inserted in a porcelain container. The tapering vase shape and its narrowed neck hold the materials in position without mechanical aid.

LILY AND *Curculigo capitulata*

A religious statue of exquisite detail from Barcelona is centered amid a profusion of lily blooms. Large flowers rise to more narrowed forms and tapering buds. Leaf blades of the Australian weevil plant through height give appropriate scale to the figure of Saint Anthony.

LILY OF THE VALLEY (*Convallaria majalis*)

Sprays and leaves of the valley lily rest in a small alabaster vase. The erectness of blooms against the severely pointed leaves gives an etched texture to this design of high luminosity. The curling of the lower leaf placements is accomplished by inserting the stem end through its own blade.

LILY OF THE VALLEY AND AZALEA

Stems of the white azalea are arranged after the manner of natural growth. In a central placement crisp lilies of the valley rise abruptly, each stem proportionate in length to its growing height. The mouth of the container flared like a grotto suggests the cool entrance to a cave.

MAGNOLIA

In this design one branch of the magnolia tree, carefully pruned to remove numerous basal leaves from around each foliage cluster, is impaled to lean at an angle. The one perfect blossom is slightly recessed to assure a dimensional effect in this pattern of splendid beauty.

Magnolia foliage and one fully opened magnolia bloom guide the eye upward through varied forms of blossoms and glistening foliage to a narrowed bud. The blackamoor figure contributes to the rhythmic swirl of this design, which is inspired by pride in a regional past.

MARIGOLD (*Tagetes erecta*)

A colorful design indicates the dominance of the large yellow marigolds when employed with their own foliage. The power and the strength that the pattern expresses are accomplished through repetition of diagonal lines.

MARIGOLD AND LEAVES

This frequently overlooked commonplace garden flower affords vividness of color, stimulating form, and thrilling texture. When arranged with a discriminate refinement, the marigold can be startling and beautiful. Leaves of the terrestrial orchid have been cut and furled to stabilize this design of signal interest.

MONDO (*Ophiopogon japonicus*)

This miniature is an excellent example of textural relationship and scale. Eight small sprays of the mondo and delicate fern tips spring up in fountain spray from a diminutive hobnail dish in this free-standing design.

MONDO WITH SMALL FLOWERS

A small perfume bottle is the container for this design of mondo, a tuberose spike, oleander blossoms, and Queen Anne's lace. Texture, pattern, and form are as clearly noted in this miniature as they would be for a design planned on a larger scale.

NASTURTIUM (*Tropæolum coccineum*)

As warm and cheerful as a summer day is this arrangement of nasturtium blooms and foliage. One long tendril of the plant dips out in an undulating, horizontal line. Bloom spikes in a rounded form suggest a rhythm of basket and disklike leaves.

Nasturtium and Leaves

Totally unlike the preceding plate is this design employing the same rhythmic line. Leaves of the agapanthus swirl upward from a rounded container. Two loquat leaves and nasturtium blooms massed at a slight angle finish the arrangement.

Oleander (*Nerium oleander*)

An unusual vase with glaze dripped on its iron core supports the molded forms of the oleander blooms. The relationship apparent between the flowers and the vase is strongly beautiful.

Oleander and Pentstemon (*Pentstemon gloxinioides*)

Pentstemon, inverted amaryllis leaves, and oleander blossoms are the subjects of this arrangement. Complete defoliation and immersion of the oleander is necessary to prolong its living beauty.

Palm (*Washingtonia filifera*)

The leaves of the fan palm have been trimmed and arranged in helical spirals to give a strong dimensional effect. The heavy pottery container offers strong support to this massive study.

Palm and Eucalyptus

Palm fronds radiate in three lines simulating their basic form. The vivid green of the palm leaves is equaled in color strength by the strong massing of the brilliant red eucalyptus stamens and bracts.

Palo Verde (*Cercidium torreyanum*)

For desert dwellers the gray palo verde tree affords highly decorative plant material indigenous to the area. One branch of the thorny plant has been thinned to distinguish two levels. Massed on the right is a low placement of white and dried desert holly. A wood fragment completes the setting.

Palo Verde with Accessories

In this arrangement of festive design the palo verde is combined with the copper-painted leaves of the bird of paradise. Foliage-green satin ribbon looped and caught in the thorny branches flows upward. Clusters of shiny copper ornaments give highlights and continuity to the burnished surfaces of the leaves.

Pandanus (*Pandanus veitchi*)

Three blades of the highly variegated screw pine flow from out a clear glass cylinder in an austere arc. One wide blade placed low within the container is congruent to the vase. Two low leaf blades curve downward, their tips completing the crescent in this design.

Pandanus and Agapanthus

Four pandanus leaves, their ends knotted, dominate this design. On the left ribbed and overlaid leaves of Dieffenbachia swirl upward. Massed umbels of agapanthus complete the arrangement. The color scheme is lavender and yellow-green.

PELARGONIUM (*Pelargonium domesticum*)

This old-fashioned garden flower offers a delicacy of form and exquisite striation in color. One tall and fluffy column of blossoms and foliage is repeated by a shorter one on the right. Blush-pink blooms streaked with crimson harmonize with a container of similar color.

PELARGONIUM AND IVY

A massing of pelargonium blooms is arranged simply and effectively with ivy leaves. This flower, like its cousin the geranium, should be picked in opening-bud stage. Complete defoliation unmasks the fragile beauty of its blossom.

PEONY (*Pæonia*)

Peonies because of their coarse foliage lend themselves well to arrangements in baskets. This same flower when completely defoliated takes on an appearance of both refinement and lushness. Buds and flower stand in dignified position, although in structural harmony with the receptacle.

PEONY AND ASPIDISTRA

Three variegated aspidistra leaves stand in reverse with their backs to the viewer. Other leaves low at the left brace and outline an ascending spiral of peony blooms. The white blossoms in the white container combine with the leaves in a monochromatic design in green.

PERUVIAN LILY (*Alstroemeria aurantiaca*)

This dainty little yellow-and-brown-flecked flower lends itself to charming arrangement in this small glass container that shows hues of amber and cream. Numerous stems are vertically placed with a fuller massing of the delicate blooms at the base of the design.

PERUVIAN LILIES AND GERBERA (*Gerbera jamesoni*)

An amber-glass cake stand with stem cavity holds water and supports the Peruvian lilies and orange gerbera. The narrowness of the stem opening firmly holds in place the floral materials independent of mechanical aid.

PETUNIA (*Petunia hybrida*)

The placements of the three main lines are composed of single varieties of petunia flowers and buds, with several blooms of the ruffled type centered at the lip of the vase. All or partial defoliation of the stem enhances petunia arrangements.

The ruffled and double types of the petunia are arranged in a softened diagonal line. The floral colors range from lavender, through orchid, to intense red-violet. The darkest tone is placed at the axis of the design. The color of the container is a purple rarely seen in glazes.

PINE (*Pinus*)

One long spray of pine is placed in a flowing curve edged by sparkling green plastic fringette along the outer rib of the branch. A large purple candle and clusters of artificial grapes complete and stabilize this design planned for a festive occasion.

PINE AND RHODODENDRON

Two sprays of pine curtsy toward one another. The rhododendron blossom, outlined by its own leaves, rests in exquisite detail low in the container. Environmental habits of growth have suggested the combining of these two materials.

PITCHER PLANT (*Sarracenia purpurea*)

This material growing wild in the moist regions of the southern United States is fascinating in both form and color. So strange is the form that for most people it needs interpretation. The fluted, conical shapes are leaves, and the puffed, rounded heads are blooms. In this design the zigzag line of leaves is softened by a contradictory line of four blossoms.

An arrangement of the sarracenia after its habit of growth depicts numerous leaves in many stages of development springing from the moist, grassy sod. One open blossom completes the cycle. A jagged stump of a tree is placed in the foreground to authenticate further the realistic setting.

PLUM (*Prunus pissardi*)

A heavy Chinese leaden scoop with jade-encrusted handle makes an appropriate container for the Oriental plum. Two fruit-bearing sprays—one erect and slightly curved; the other reaching to the table—establish the main lines of the design. A massing of fruit forms gives stability.

PLUM AND CASTOR BEAN

The container has a shiny, mahogany-colored finish. Red-brown sprays of ornamental plum foliage are combined with the burgundy colors of the castor bean; rich leaves, two

bud spikes, and opening flowers make this a monochrome of muted tones.

PRINCESS FLOWER (*Tibouchina semidecandra*)

This royal purple flower contributes outstanding color to the garden or an arrangement. Its felted dentate leaves match the gray-green of the container in this simple design of one leafy spray showing flowers and buds. A few blooms outlined by leaves form the base of the design.

PRINCESS FLOWER AND CLOVER (*Trifolium incarnatum*)

In a ribbed and flaring red-violet bowl the purest of purple-hued princess flowers are massed in a cone. The paraboloid is completed by container and teakwood base. To the left is a casual placement of the clover in coloring identical with that of the vase. These rounded heads give variation to the other geometrical forms.

PRIVET (*Ligustrum ovalifolium*)

The golden privet with its graceful and geometrical spacing of leaves lends itself to lovely patterned effects alone or as background material. A container with a flaring base supports numerous stalks of the shrub.

PRIVET AND CHRYSANTHEMUMS

Here, as background material, the yellow and green variegated privet flows upward in a soft arc. Small, yellow-green chrysanthemums follow the established dominant line. The combination of these two materials assures a long-lasting design. The container is a medium value of harmonizing color.

PYRACANTHA (*Pyracantha lalandi*)

In a Chinese copper container a spray of the pyracantha, heavy with vibrant orange berries, extends from one side of the vase. Only one branch was deftly pruned and placed at an angle to make this an outstanding composition for sheer simplicity.

PYRACANTHA AND CELOSIA

Three sprays of orange-berried pyracantha in flowing curves are placed in the rich yellow container as though braced against the wind. Even the plumed yellow celosia at their base is blown in the same direction. This latter detail gives this design a consistency of idea and rhythm.

QUEEN ANNE'S LACE (*Daucus carota*)

A basket fashioned from split bamboo affords an airiness of woven pattern completely appropriate to the delicacy and rounded heads of the Queen Anne's lace. Two tall floral spikes repeat the line of the handle. The five lower blooms, although erect, repeat the circular line of the receptacle.

QUEEN ANNE'S LACE AND FERN

A cranberry-red round glass container mounted on a crystal pedestal gives support and complementary color to this ebullient design of Queen Anne's lace and tufts of wild fern fronds. These plant materials were gathered from the side of the road.

RHODODENDRON

Three masses of umbellated form of this flower are arranged alone. A gradation in the size of each cluster from the basal bloom upward is subtle in plan. The fragility of the blossoms demands an unusual refinement in the container, which is satisfied by this thin pottery.

RHODODENDRON AND *Melianthus major*

The grayed leaves of the melianthus major give background tracery in this composition emphasized by a striated piece of gray driftwood placed diagonally in the design. Rose-tinted blooms of the rhododendron impart a dusty softness to this portrayal.

ROCKS

Since the time of primitive man rocks have played an integral part in his life. Not only were they used for physical needs, but the awesomeness of rock forms and jagged peaks evoked worshipful reverence. In this design rocks selected for form and color are placed in a grouping of three levels with bits of teardrop moss draping their sides and wedged in the crevices.

ROCKS WITH PINE

The large container of crude brown clay supports groupings of rocks and holds water necessary to the life of the evergreen material. One rock teeters precariously, eroded by wind. Branches of pine are placed in a seemingly casual manner high in the composition simulating the altitude of their normal growth. The lower spiked forms are reeds arranged realistically in the wet marsh of the low plain, adjacent to the snows of this setting.

ROSE (*Rosa*)

This arrangement of roses is an excellent example of the elements of line, form, texture, pattern, and color apparent in good design. Six yellow-orange roses with their green foliage grace an amber-colored glass vase.

Rose with Other Flowers

The form of a delicate glass brandy-snifter supports the softened crescent line of this dainty pattern employing tiny sprays of the hedge myrtle, miniature roses, and one flowered umbel of the Queen Anne's lace. The definitive form and clarity of outline of each material used emphasize the importance of pattern in design.

Sansevieria (*Sansevieria thyrsiflora*)

The strap form of these flecked and reptilian leaves adapts itself to brilliant design. Six leaves are cut different lengths and placed firmly erect. A seventh leaf is looped and its blade placed diagonally to give a flourish of completion. No water is required.

Sansevieria and Anthurium

With its leathery sheen the snake plant harmonizes with the textured brilliance of the anthurium. Two glossy leaves of the monstera find diagonal placement in this design of tropical materials.

Spathiphyllum

One dark-green ovoid leaf of this plant is centered in the design and two leaves angle slightly to the right. The lower leaf, its upper portion rolled, curves into the other leaf with a continuation of the rib line. The spathes and floral bracts of the spathiphyllum furl upward from the luminous glass container.

Spathiphyllum and Strelitzia (*Strelitzia nicolai*)

This arrangement of exotic materials is presented in spectacular design. One large stalk with three black bracts and white-crested blooms of the traveler's palm, or strelitzia nicolai, is placed on the left. Five spathes of the spathiphyllum are assembled as one magnificent flower.

Stock (*Mathiola incana*)

In a powder-pink bowl sprays of double stock reflecting the same color are vertically arranged. Twin floral spikes step upward, giving indentation and interesting silhouette to the composition. Overlapping leaves from this plant repeat the floral line.

Stock and Cabbage

A slab of rare wood with a deep pocket for water and flower holder is used for this arrangement of orchid stock and richly colored red-violet cabbage. The textural transition from the slab into the basal placement of furled leaves is particularly noticeable in this design.

Strelitzia (*Strelitzia reginæ*)

The stately leaves of this plant with its own blooms make a highly stylized display. Three frontal leaves face the viewer. Three leaves, folded, silhouette the undersides of the foliage. Four blossoming stalks are so placed that they repeat the line of the grouping on the left.

Strelitzia and Tropical Fruit

The orange bird of paradise, angular in form and showy in color, combines well with tropical fruits of distinctive shape. The pineapple, long a favored source for design, fingers of bananas, and the dried and curled leaf of the pandanus give form and color to this arrangement in its wooden bowl.

SUCCULENTS

Succulent plant materials when arranged without water last for months. A tall spike of succulent growth is placed erect and turned so the angular lines are evident. Two varieties of æonium are stacked in triangular fashion at the entrance of the vase.

SUCCULENTS AND SANSEVIERIA

This design of sansevieria and aloe is fantastically similar in color marking and tactile harmony. Six serrated fronds of another variety of aloe are placed on the right; some are looped on the left. Here again water, if used, would hasten deterioration of the plant material. The container is heavy pottery in keeping with this strong, fibrous design.

SUNFLOWER (*Helianthus annus*)

Wild sunflowers picked in the open fields are arranged in an appropriate tawny container. These flowers should be selected while in opening-bud stage. Almost complete defoliation and deep immersion will eliminate any odor or disagreeable sap flow usually connected with this flower.

SUNFLOWER AND DOCK (*Rumex*)

A rustic tree stump placed in a wooden bowl suggests the line of the plant materials. Roadside dock, dark brown in color, flares out at the left, duplicating the boot form of the tree. Other stalks end in a terminal spike.

Sunflowers, stripped of foliage, curve up into a vertical line in this brown and yellow study.

SWEET PEA (*Lathyrus odoratus*)

A unique hand-blown green bottle is the receptacle for three clustered sprays of sweet pea blooms. The curved vine at the apex of the composition repeats the recessed pattern near the base of the container. One long pendent spray parallels the neck of the bottle in this design employing popular plant material.

SWEET PEA AND GERANIUM LEAVES (*Pelargonium*)

Pale pink and deeper rose-pink sweet peas complete the soft flowing arc originated by the leaves of the peppermint geranium. The lowest spray of sweet peas was accomplished by entwining shorter-stemmed placements to the longest floral spike, using it as a support, before inserting it as a unit in a round, pedestaled, green glass container.

TUBEROSE (*Polyanthes tuberosa*)

In a gold compote of graceful vertical proportion and restrained flaring rim a free-standing arrangement of tuberose lends related elegance. These ivory-colored flowers, each blossom as though carved, are given patterned silhouette by their blush-pink tips.

TUBEROSE AND DILL (*Anethum graveolens*)

An open lacework white Sèvres fruit bowl shields an inconspicuous container for water and holder. The swirl of the dolphin-figured base is beautifully repeated by the two lines of tuberose. Wild dill, lacelike and airy, repeats the pattern of the container.

TULIP

White tulips with their grayed green foliage are placed off center in a bowl of the same green apparent in the leaves. Each flower and leaf establishes a perfect pattern: nothing to be added, nothing to be deleted. Absence of crossing lines gives purity of form to this arrangement.

TULIP WITH DAFFODILS AND IRIS

A fan-shaped design flares from out a black glass container supported by a heavy crystal ball. The container itself is fan-shaped. Daffodils compose the softened lateral placements, and yellow irises crest the rosetted mass of fully opened yellow tulip blossoms in this monochromatic arrangement.

VEGETABLES

The disklike forms of summer squash and purple onions suggest to the arranger a design planned to display these shapes advantageously. Three squash and one onion are impaled on small sticks and inserted in the holder. One onion rests on its side. Wax beans flare out fan-fashion on the right, while others on the left whirl into and over the basal squash, which was added low for color reflection and repetition of form.

Three cucumbers impaled vertically on sticks suggest a diagonal plan. Two summer squash angularly placed on the right definitely establish it. A firmly centered placement of one large purple onion, a pale-green squash, and purple eggplant with green-tinted stem and crown contribute to a design of vigorous form and color. Leaves of red cabbage are placed in opposition to the dominant line.

WATER LILY (*Nymphæa*)

Water lilies are arranged in a realistic manner. Each unit of the plant's growth is a studied placement; each form is employed only and if it will contribute to the cycle of the grouped material. Since all plants grow toward light, the position of the sun is denoted by the tipped buds, leaves, and blooms. A tree stump further authenticates this swamp scene.

WATER LILY AND CANE GRASS

Striped cane grass fringing the edge of the marsh stands erect behind a water lily assembled after its true manner of growth. This realistic design is further authenticated by the large ivory-colored container from Japan, typifying Oriental style of floral art.

YUCCA

In this design there is a quality of smartness which was achieved by simplicity of linear plan and the plant materials employed. Two clipped palm fronds rest in a lateral position, although their leaf structure is diagonal. Sprays of waxen and exquisite yucca blooms repeat this line. One palm blade on the right reassures the horizontal form of the composition and the bamboo segment.

YUCCA AND LEAVES

One tall and massive stalk of the yucca, dignified in appearance, is placed in a container of proportionate size. Two large leaves of the traveler's palm encircle and hold high as a *torchère* the Lord's Candle. For purposes of design the yucca blossoms rest low at the base. In the realm of imagination this repetition of floral color might be waxen droplets from this stately flare.

ZINNIA

Red-orange zinnias arranged in a green container lined with a similar red-orange tone give effective complementary color. These brilliant and cheerful flowers require almost complete defoliation and deep immersion for their conditioning. Unless so treated they tend to wilt rapidly. This design repeats triangular patterns throughout the composition, even in foliage detail.

ZINNIA AND BARLEY (*Hordeum vulgare*)

A garden hat with an inner receptacle is crushed in a casual manner to display an arrangement consistent with the informality of the container. The midsummer sun has already matured the tawny barley sprays, and the vivid yellow, orange, and red zinnias are in their glory.

A NOTE ON THE TYPE

The text of this book was set on the Linotype in ELECTRA, *designed by* W. A. DWIGGINS. *The Electra face is a simple and readable type suitable for printing books by present-day processes. It is not based on any historical model, and hence does not echo any particular time or fashion. It is without eccentricities to catch the eye and interfere with reading—in general, its aim is to perform the function of a good book printing-type: to be read, and not seen.*

The book was composed, printed, and bound by KINGSPORT PRESS, *Inc., Kingsport, Tennessee. Color reproductions from* CHANTICLEER COMPANY, *New York. Black-and-white halftones from* CAPPER ENGRAVING COMPANY, *Knoxville, Tennessee.*

Typography by SIDNEY R. JACOBS. *Binding design and special initials by* CHARLES E. SKAGGS.